TRAVELS
MY TUBA
My Life in Music

JIM ANDERSON

APS Books
Yorkshire

APS Books,
The Stables Field Lane, Aberford, West Yorkshire LS25 3AE

APS Books is a subsidiary of the
APS Publications imprint

www.andrewsparke.com

First published worldwide by APS Books in 2021

A catalogue record for this book is available from the British Library

ISBN 978-1-78996-431-8

INTRODUCTION

All of my professional life I have been given money for blowing down a length of brass tubing. I have done this with most of the orchestras in the UK and many international ones, including the London Symphony Orchestra, London Philharmonic Orchestra, Royal Philharmonic Orchestra and Boston Symphony Orchestra. I was a member of the BBC Symphony Orchestra, the Orchestra of the Age of Enlightenment, the Wallace Collection and the London Sinfonietta.

I have worked under the baton of many Sirs: Adrian Boult, Malcolm Sergeant, Antonio Pappano, Colin Davis, George Solti, Simon Rattle; and many non-Sirs: Aaron Copland, Benjamin Britten, Seiji Ozawa, Bernard Haitink, Leonard Bernstein, Mariss Jansons. I was Mr Oom-Pah-Pah in *Rainbow* with Bungle and Zippy – one of the most famous children's programmes in the 1970s – and Tubby the Tuba, in another. I have played on the soundtrack of many films – Bond films, *Star Wars*, *Lord of the Rings*. My playing has accompanied episodes of *Poirot* and *Mr Bean*. I was the tuba professor at the Guildhall School of Music and Drama for 30 years.

I have been amazingly lucky, and I have had a thoroughly good time. I wanted to give my professional musician's insight into the world of music before the memories disappear into the mists of my brain.

CHAPTER 1

OVERTURE ...

The last notes of Mahler's 8th Symphony, the 'Symphony of a Thousand', faded away into that vast unique silence of the Royal Albert Hall. One thousand people – a hundred players on the stage, and a choir of nine hundred. We all held our collective breaths, knowing that we had made great music together. The conductor slowly lowered his baton. Then the total silence was shattered by the roaring applause of the six thousand-strong audience. Pierre Boulez, the conductor, gave each section a bow. Woodwind first, then percussion, strings, brass: trumpets, horns, trombones, and the tuba (me)!

For all performers, the end of a concert is a release of anxieties and a time for reflection. I thought how lucky I was to do this remarkable job, and the bizarre way it had all started.

... AND BEGINNERS

I was born in Moss Side, the youngest of three. The name suggests sylvan streams flowing through mossy banks. In fact, it was a very poor area of industrial Manchester. From infancy I suffered from bronchiectasis – a severe bronchitic complaint – and my early memories were of having to stay home whenever there were smogs, which was often. These were a mixture of toxic smoke and fog. Every winter they saw off the elderly and those with respiratory conditions: consequently, I missed a lot of school.

My memories of my dad at that time, nine years after he had got home from the war, were that he wanted to live abroad. Canada or Tasmania featured most regularly in his conversations, but the list was long. After a while we assumed that he just liked daydreaming and talking about 'abroad' as some kind of fictional place of milk and honey, a place where dreams come true. He had a good job working for Kellogg's looking after their machines. One day his boss called him in and asked if he wanted to set up and run a new factory in Cape Town. This seemed to be an answer to his prayers. He would go to Cape Town, live there for three to four months, find a house and then we would all emigrate. A much better salary, a lovelier climate. He accepted the offer.

My mum wasn't keen, but my dad was unstoppable. Very soon, wearing smart clothes and carrying a new suitcase, he said goodbye to us, promising he would write. I was nine, my brother fourteen and my sister eighteen.

I had always felt close to my dad and I really missed him. For the first two months we received enthusiastic letters about lovely houses, lots of money and a great lifestyle. Then two more months passed and…nothing. I began to fear I'd never see him again.

After five months the phone rang. My dad was at Manchester Ringway Airport. Could my mum go to collect him because he didn't have enough money for his bus fare home. The man she brought home was thin, shabby and suitcase-less. Whatever had happened in his time away was never mentioned by anybody and remained a family mystery. Years later I asked him in private about that time. I said I reckoned he had fallen in lust with someone who had spent his cash. He looked at me, smiled and said, 'That's what you reckoned?' He never said another word about it – ever.

With my dad home, the house was even more overcrowded. There were eight of us: my nan, two *Barnado's* ladies whom my nan had taken in, my mum, dad and three kids – in a three-bedroom house! On our doctor's recommendation – but mostly because of my lung condition – we were given a council house in Poynton, away from the polluted air. My breathing became easier, I put on weight and for the first time in my life I began to feel well.

I took my 11-plus exam. All children had to take this exam; if they passed then they were eligible to go to a grammar school; if they failed, they were sent to a secondary modern school.

I failed, so I went to 'that secondary school', as my mother called it. Both my sister and my brother had passed their 11-plus exams, and went to the grammar school. My mother never missed an opportunity to remind me of their success and my lack of it. As it transpired, failing this exam and going to 'that school' was to change my life.

THE SCHOOL BAND

I was ten when I met my first brass instrument, a trombone my brother had brought home from school. The fascination was immediate and profound. He showed me how to blow it, I tried it and loved it and I begged him to keep it. I pleaded with my parents for a trombone, a trumpet, any brass instrument. Money was short, but they did buy me a plastic trumpet with a reed in the mouthpiece and four valves, which played the same note when pressed.

An older boy on our street had a real trumpet and invited me round to have a go. I was just beginning to get a sense of it when he started making lewd suggestions to me, at which point I handed back the trumpet and scarpered.

When I was fourteen, my big sister and her husband bought a large, run-down Victorian house, which I was quick to explore. Up in the attic, among the dusty photos, broken fire-guards and general junk, I found a tarnished-black, small, silver-plated tuba.

They say timing is everything, and I found that tuba just when my school wanted to start a brass band. I washed it out in the bath and bought some silver polish. By the time I'd finished, the bath and I were covered in 40 years of blackened tarnished silver, while the battered tuba gleamed in my hands.

I was considered musical for two reasons: I was in the choir and I played in a skiffle group – complete with a tea-chest bass and a washboard – but our family's true, unrecognised talent was my sister. I didn't know this for years – not until she shyly gave me a CD that somebody had recorded of her singing, and I heard how lovely her voice was, and how expressive her phrasing.

At the school dance, I sang and played the guitar – as did many others: it was a good shortcut into music as many of the songs of the day could be accompanied (more or less) by three chords and you didn't need to be able to read music. These were the days of a Scotsman living in London called Lonnie Donegan. He brought us lots of energetic songs from America.

I took my tuba to school, and played a few notes to our music master. They said they wanted to buy it, gave me £5 to give to my sister and told me that I was 'in the band'. I was given a fingering chart – a one-octave C scale, with numbers nought to three written under each note. These denoted which of the three valves to press in order, nought being no valves, to (theoretically) get the notes. I was told to learn the scale, and that there would be a band practice every Monday.

Considering the fact that we were all beginners, we made good progress and after three months played our first gig, at our school's Christmas concert.

I'd played a solo – a song written for bass/baritone called 'In Cellar Cool' or 'Drinking' (a favourite pursuit of brass players, according to some string players). The conductor of the local village band was at the concert and asked me to join.

By now, I wanted to play the euphonium. The euphonium, or tenor tuba, is smaller than the bass tuba: it is to the brass band what a heroic tenor is to the opera. I wanted the glamour of it – to play tunes and countermelodies, not just the bass lines like the relatively unromantic, bigger tuba. However, whenever I played the bass tuba, everybody said how great it sounded. Given that I wasn't much good at anything else, this praise was enough to keep me tied to the bass tuba.

A few months later, the band gave a concert at a Salvation Army meeting house. As usual I was to play my solo, 'Drinking' (for the teetotal Salvation Army...). We arrived at the hall, climbed the stage, and realised there were no music stands. Joe Wyche, our headmaster, who had a fairly short fuse at the best of times, began to rant. One of the quicker-witted SA Generals jumped up and said 'Fear not – our children will be the music stands. God will provide.' My nerves were increased when I found my music stand was beside one of the biggest girls I had ever seen. She towered over me and smiled and winked at me all the way through my solo.

CONTESTS

I was really enjoying my banding, and through them, I was introduced to the world of march contests. Contesting is a strange phenomenon in the brass band world. In most contests all the bands play the same test piece. It is incredibly partisan, and seems to involve strengthening band loyalty while increasing hatred of all of the band's competitors. At the end of competitions, when the results and scores are announced, we hear 'We were robbed. We deserved to win.' Strangely this animosity seems essential to the whole world of banding and somehow unites everyone. Much like football, really.

We went on a trip to London with my local band – my first trip ever. We went to play in the annual contests for all of the bands in Britain at Hammersmith Town Hall, along with all the other fourth section bands. We didn't get any prizes... We were robbed!

The contest for the first section bands (think of them as the equivalent to the premier division in football) always takes place at the Royal Albert Hall. The bands who win the first four places in the contest of the day combine to give a concert there in the evening. This is every bandsman's highlight of the year. I remember arriving late for the concert and running up the stone steps to the balcony of the Albert Hall with the sounds of Liszt's *Les Préludes* (played by the four Championship bands) pouring down on us, like a sound waterfall. It was exhilarating.

We stayed at the De Vere Hotel, Kensington, which cost thirty-eight shillings (about £1.80 in new money) a night. My parents were appalled at the expense and whenever I crossed the line, or was deemed not to be pulling my weight at home, my father would say, 'You're not staying in that London hotel now you know.'

My mate Les Hall was a fine cornet player and we had both begun playing in the village band at about the same time. Les was a few years older than me and was serving as an apprenticed toolmaker with Mirrlees Works, which made diesel engines for trains. His works band had vacancies for a cornet and a euphonium player. Their main attraction for me was that the band paid their players a small fee for rehearsals and concerts; it seemed a lot for an impecunious fifteen-year-old, so I joined. I became their second euphonium player, vowing that I was never going to play the tuba again.

All the band members – old men of thirty – welcomed me. They often took me for a pint after the rehearsal, but as I didn't like beer then, I asked them for an alternative recommendation. One of them suggested port and lemon, and from then on, the round of drinks was several pints of bitter and a port and lemon, usually served in a fluted sherry glass. It was always given to me with great solemnity and seemingly always done with kindness – if they were laughing at me it was in a good friendly way. For a year, I went along happily playing euphonium with them. Then the day arrived for us to play in the Annual March Contests.

To an outsider they were and remain strange affairs but they're a tradition of the brass band world. The contests were usually held around the time of the Whitsuntide holidays, usually the end of May. All the local northern churches held Whitsuntide Walks. The congregation of each church or chapel would put on their Sunday best, and with their banners, crucifixes and various religious artefacts, would march behind the band they had employed. This usually happened in the mornings and often three or four bands would play different marches within earshot, sounding like something Charles Ives, who composed *Putnam's Camp*, might put together.

In the afternoons, when the bands had finished their processions, they would compete in march contests. These contests were held in lots of small towns and this is what happened. A band would wait in marching order. On the signal they would march into the town square, then wait again. A whistle would be blown from an open window. The judges sat behind the curtains of one of the houses in the square, as they weren't supposed to know which band was playing. The band would play its contest march, march away, and be replaced by the next band. The results were given later in the day. Then the bands would board their coaches and drive to the next contest (often via a pub) in an adjacent town.

The first of these march contests I ever played in was with Poynton, my local band. The band secretary, Albert Hall, was a dispiriting old man. Everything seemed to make him miserable – especially people under the age of fifty. The fact that he had the same name as the famous concert hall had given him the delusion of musical credibility, even though he couldn't play an instrument. He would open the band hut, clean it, make sure the heating was working, and put the music on the stands; so in this respect he was invaluable. His reward, as far as he saw it, was to play the bass drum on all of the band's marching dates. The night before the first march, our band conductor would send Albert out of the rehearsal on some pretext, then say to the band 'Just one word of advice, ignore the bass drum tomorrow.' This is rather difficult as marches can't be conducted, so the bass drum is the time-keeper, giving the band four bars of rhythm before they play:

 PLAY

Dum-dum, rest. Dum-dum, rest. Dum, dum, dum, rest. Play!

But Albert had no sense of rhythm. On the day, we lined up in marching order at the top of the hill. Albert stood proudly on the back row wearing the band's bass drum. Eschewing a harness specially designed for the job, he used a piece of rope. As the signal to start the march was given, he thumped out two beats, the drum broke free from its moorings and rolled down the steep hill, scattering bandsmen left and right.

'So that's what they mean by a drum roll,' said one of our band.

The following year I was playing with Mirrlees band for their march contests. One Sunday none of their tuba players had turned up, so there was no bass line. The instruments were in the bus, but not the players. Les, my mate, told them that I played the tuba well, so I was given two instruments to try.

The first felt fine, but the second was great. I felt excited and certain I would enjoy it. This was my instrument and I was going to own it. It was a spring day and I was outside in the fresh air in the Pennines: everything felt right. Throughout the day, members of the band encouraged me. 'That's your instrument, lad, you sound marvellous on it. You know you should be playing it all the time, don't you?'

I knew they were right: the euphonium had never felt as good as this.

I began to discover how wonderfully satisfying it was to play a good bass line, to provide a foundation for the band to sit on. I was to discover later that providing a foundation for a whole symphony orchestra, to give a springboard for melodies to soar into the heights, was even better. The tuba also has one great advantage over the euphonium: it is a regular member of larger symphony orchestras. Wagner's *Ring* cycle, Bruckner and Mahler symphonies, there's a long list of great bass parts for the tuba. Even the odd solo.

CHAPTER 2

DISCOVERING ORCHESTRAS

While still enjoying the sound of bands, my interest in orchestras was growing. We had a 'Dansette Major' record player and a few records at home. The first one I bought was an LP of *The King and I* but I quickly moved on to operatic arias. I had an EP (extended player single) of the aria 'One Fine Day' from Puccini's *Madame Butterfly*. I wasn't allowed to play it when my father was at home: it was one of the five records he had owned when he was stationed in India during the war, and he couldn't listen to it without experiencing emotions too strong for words. A recording of *From the New World* (Dvorak's 9th Symphony) followed, and then a classic recording of Beethoven's 5th Symphony with the Concertgebouw Orchestra, conducted by Erich Kleiber, which is still my favourite.

I became fixated by the sound of the violin after hearing Mendelssohn's Violin Concerto. I was transported by the sheer beauty of it. On the recording I bought, the violin soloist was Alfredo Campoli. I was to meet him a few years later.

Meanwhile, as I was discovering orchestras and solo violin recordings, I met a local girl from the posher part of our town, who played the violin. She told me that she was in the Cheshire Youth Orchestra and that they held an annual residential week's course. I contacted them and discovered they needed a tuba player.

I decided to go on the course – spurred on by my unreciprocated attraction to my violin-playing friend – but the second I sat in the first rehearsal, I found out what true love was. I was instantly smitten. If there really is a 'road to Damascus' experience, this was mine.

Here was a whole spectrum of many more different sounds and colours: the sounds of strings, woodwind and brass, combined wonderfully by composers with fantastic skills and often with genius. On first hearing Schubert's *Rosamunde*, sitting listening to the rehearsal surrounded by strings and woodwind, I was transported and I knew that, more than anything else, I wanted to be a part of this. The problem was I would need some O-levels.

FURTHER EDUCATION?

My secondary modern school finished teaching its students when they became 15, and so didn't cover the O-level (currently GCSE) syllabus.

I enrolled at a newly established College of Further Education. When I did my interview for them, I had been assured that I could add music and French to my subjects. When I started at the college, I enquired about this and was told that it wouldn't be possible for me to do either of these subjects as no one else in the class wanted to take them.

From the start, the college was a disaster. There didn't seem to be a timetable or any indication of where the students were to go for their lessons. Day-release students turned up from their firms to smoke, swear and enjoy their day away from work. Judging by the noise we heard from some of the other classrooms, teachers were being abused, and there was a huge turnover of staff. Over the two-year course, we saw several supply teachers in all of our subjects come and go. The worst case was in the science department. We had seven science teachers in that two years.

The last teacher arrived six weeks before the final biology exam. She questioned us about what we had covered and became increasingly horrified by our total lack of knowledge. In a brave attempt to achieve something, she told us she was very good at spotting possible exam questions.

She predicted we'd be asked to dissect a worm, so we spent several weeks practising. The day of the exam arrived and we watched the colour drain from her cheeks when she opened the box of specimens. We soon realised why. The earthworms we were expecting were nowhere to be seen. In their place were shrimps. We all failed.

The geography teacher, Robert-Smythe (Bob Smith?), was also the vice-principal of this mess of a place. He was a poser – complete with Hush Puppies and a sports jacket with leather elbow patches. He gave the impression that he couldn't wait to move, with his hyphen and his cravat, to somewhere more fitting of his station.

When I first talked to him, I unwisely let slip that I loved to play the tuba. One warm afternoon as the geography class was becoming (even more) comatose as he droned on, he suddenly said 'Anderson, what's a Jurassic escarpment?'

I replied 'I don't know, sir.'

'You don't know! I suppose you think you are going to make a living playing that tuba of yours? Eh, class?' He waited hopefully for the sycophantic laughter that didn't follow. He repeated his joke many times, and I vowed that if I ever did get a job playing 'that tuba of mine', he would be the first person I'd tell.

Some of the students passed a few exams, many failed them all. I passed English and woodwork. It had been a waste of two years. I felt cross with myself for making a bad choice and I still had no qualifications. Playing music became even more important to me; I considered it the only thing I could do.

I finished my week's course with the Cheshire Youth Orchestra. We brass players were lucky enough to have Ken Monks, a horn player from the Liverpool Philharmonic Orchestra, as our tutor. He was an enthusiast and I hung on to his every word. After a couple of days, he told me I had potential and said that if I wanted to forge a career as a tuba player, I'd have to go to music college.

He thought that the Royal Manchester College of Music (now the Royal Northern College of Music), might need a tuba student. The new term was starting in six weeks and though I was late to apply, luck was on my side. The trombone and tuba professor, Terry Nagle, phoned me and said that if I could play well enough, he would consider me for a place at the college. I would have to do an audition, playing two contrasting pieces. I had very little knowledge of orchestral tuba repertoire and I didn't want to play a brass band piece, in case it marked me as 'just a bandsman', so I searched for two good audition pieces.

Having recently heard Mozart's 4th horn concerto, I decided I would play its last, fast movement, which would show off my technique. Thinking 'Nagle' sounded Welsh (he was), I would also play 'Land Of My Fathers' – a slow piece to show off my sound.

There was now the problem of approaching my father. I had worked on a farm in most of my school holidays, and I had already applied for a place at an agricultural college, which he was pleased about. I told him all of the good things about being in an orchestra. He listened with increasing impatience, then said, 'No son of mine is going to be an itinerant musician.'

After I'd stressed the fact that the college of music course would qualify me to teach, he was slightly mollified and reluctantly agreed that I could at least do the audition.

FAMILY LIFE

My brother and sister, five and nine years older than me, were afraid of our dad, but I had a good relationship with him. I had been born the year after the war ended – a baby boomer. The family's home life during the war had been, with the exception of my brother, all women. They were ill prepared for the small angry man who had crashed into their relatively organised and comfortable world at the end of the war. My brother told me his first memory of our father was when he saw a man in the street looking into the house through the curtains. On our dad's first night in the house my brother wouldn't get undressed in front of him, and told my mum, 'Tell that man to go away.' Both he and my sister were locked out of Mum's life from then. Occasionally, when he got angry, he would hit them.

Our dad had spent his childhood in the slums. He was one of seven; his father had abandoned them, disappearing without trace. My mum had had a similarly hard life and was often beaten by her unpredictable stepmother.

They had got married when they were both sixteen. My sister was born six months later, and my brother five years after that. Two years later my dad, dressed in khaki, was on a boat to India, to fight in World War II. By a fluke he escaped being captured by the Japanese. Shortly after this, he spent two weeks on a beach in Dunkirk but a long time passed before he finally returned home. I think my mum and dad, like tens of thousands of other couples, spent their life trying to rebuild their relationship.

I was a mistake, my dad told me. I didn't mind, I felt that he approved of me somehow and he seldom hit me. I don't remember seeing him hit my brother and sister, but they said he did, and understandably they were scared of him.

Possibly because I seemed to be Dad's favourite, my mum felt she had to redress this imbalance by being more critical of me, often bringing up the subject of my failure to get into the grammar school.

I assumed that my mum had experienced a stressful war because of the rationing. When my sister was young, she was told by my mum not to mention the Americans who were stationed locally, and who were very generous. My sister said that both she and my brother were often given candy and thought all Americans were great. A few years later, my mum was telling the assembled company that she had given up sugar during the war, so that her children could have her ration. In an aside to me, my sister said, 'That doesn't explain the fact that though she was a short woman, she weighed sixteen stone at the end of the war!'

Dad had never talked about his two weeks on the beach at Dunkirk. After he retired, he and my mum came to stay with me - they had emigrated to Canada in 1965. My mum used to talk incessantly and I fancied having a quiet day out with my dad. I suggested a boat trip on the Thames, from Charing Cross to the Cutty Sark. It was a sunny day and we sat on the upper deck, watching the sights of London's landscape drifting past. I noticed that there was a brass plaque on the side of one of the boat's seats. It said that this boat had gone across the Channel to Dunkirk and had brought back many hundreds of troops. I pointed it out to my dad, and asked, 'Was this the boat that brought you back from Dunkirk, Dad?'

He didn't say anything for a while, and his eyes looked into the distance, then he started to speak. 'One of the things I remember from the beach was the smell. There was nothing to eat and water was scarce. As the wounded were given priority on the hospital boats, some of the uninjured officers used to take bloody bandages from the wounded men and put them around their own heads. We saw one of them do this and get on to a hospital ship. As it set off, it was dive-bombed and sank – we all cheered.

'I saw fifty soldiers trying to get into some of the small boats that would only have held ten people, and watched the boats sink. Often the people who had brought their boats to rescue us didn't have their identity papers with them; sometimes they were treated as spies and were shot.' Another awful, seldom-reported truth about war. That was the first and last time he spoke of it.

THE ROYAL MANCHESTER COLLEGE OF MUSIC

I did my audition at the college two weeks later, and Terry, the trombone/tuba professor, offered me a place starting the following week. I had been careful not to discuss my lack of exam qualifications and I was relieved that they didn't ask me any questions about my education. I discovered they didn't have any first-study tuba students and were very keen to get one; and they had a tuba I could borrow.

This boosted my confidence, but I was very nervous on my first day. As I climbed the steps into the imposing hallway, it felt as if everybody seemed to know each other. I was surrounded by students talking of their Special Advanced level music successes, the National Youth Orchestra and their Grade 8 distinctions. As I had never taken any grade exams, I felt out of place and wondered if I should have gone to the agricultural college after all, but before long, all of my doubts disappeared, with my involvement in the wonderfully different world of music-making.

The Royal Northern College of Music is now a splendidly equipped place, with all the latest facilities and practice rooms, concert halls and recording studios. The same couldn't be said of its predecessor that I attended, the old Royal Manchester College of Music. It had started life as a hall, with a few practice rooms mainly reserved for strings, and the quieter instruments; not brass! There were a few rooms with good pianos, which were for the better first-study pianists. As the college expanded, it needed more space for its students: terraced houses along the adjacent side street were bought and converted into makeshift practice studios. These were cramped and had very low ceilings, so playing a brass instrument in them was quite deafening. The tuba was the worst, as the bell pointed up to the low ceiling and the sound bounced right back into the room.

I turned up for my first lesson with Terry. I had never had a tuba lesson before and didn't know what to expect; should I have prepared something? Would I be able to play well enough? He was a friendly man and from the outset encouraging. My lessons with him settled down to a pattern and became very interesting. He was a good trombone player and a sound musician, but unfortunately, he had no idea of how to play the tuba. While he could tell me what was good or bad, he couldn't actually show me how to play anything, or demonstrate tuba parts. He was the 1st trombone in the Hallé Orchestra, so he did have a great knowledge of essential brass repertoire from first-hand experience. As a conscientious teacher, I think he must have often felt a bit frustrated by his inability to show me how the tuba should sound.

When he began his teaching session, he always gave me the first lesson, then he would happily teach the trombones.

Although he would never have admitted this, he just wanted to get my lesson out of the way. Terry often arrived home late after travelling from one of his evening concerts and when he turned up to teach first thing in the morning, he was sometimes tired from the night before. Unfortunately, his lessons were always in the college annexe with its small rooms and low ceilings, not a great place in which to hear enthusiastic tuba playing, and particularly not if you were feeling fragile.

On the bad days, he would tell me to play my prepared study. As I played enthusiastically, he would take out his newspaper and disappear behind it. On the really bad days, he would also light his pipe. Smoke would drift up from behind his paper and the small room would fill up with fumes. When he couldn't stand the noise of the tuba bouncing off the ceiling any more, he used to say, 'All right stop now. Let me have a go.' He would then try to blow my tuba, leaving it tasting of pipe fumes before throwing in the towel and suggesting we go for a cup of tea. Some days called for something stronger.

On one of his not-so-good days an hour's lesson might only last for about twenty minutes. Afterwards he would insist on buying us both a drink. At this point he would start to relax, telling me that the lessons were going fine, and that he would see me the following week. It wasn't the best teaching in the world, but I was grateful for any teaching at all. Luckily, during my last six months at college, I was well taught by Stuart Roebuck, who had become the tuba player in the Hallé.

The college tuba was made of unlacquered brass, which gave me a rash. A doctor said it was an allergic reaction and that I should wear cotton gloves when I played. The only cotton gloves I could find were white. They looked ridiculous, but my college mates were quite good at not laughing at me too much.

CHAPTER 3

THE HALLÉ

After four months at college, I was asked if I would like to do a concert with the Hallé Orchestra. The Hallé was 'Manchester's orchestra'. Sir John Barbirolli was their conductor so for me this was a dream come true. I was to play the 2nd tuba part in Berlioz's *Symphonie fantastique* and I practised the 'Dies Irae'. Two tubas play this dirge-like tune in the last movement of the symphony. I have since played it several hundred times.

I turned up about two hours early for my first rehearsal with the Hallé, at the Zion Institute, a huge Methodist church in the middle of a large slum area of Manchester. It was an amazingly dark grey place, and the housing that surrounded it was blackened by years of coal burning; most houses had been condemned – not a place where you would happily wander after nightfall. It was cleared many years ago.

The best way I can describe how it was then, would be to find some of the darker L. S. Lowry paintings: *Christ Church Salford*, which he painted in 1965, is a good example. Combine this with the more gothic passages of Mervyn Peake's *Gormenghast* trilogy: 'The sun sank with a sob and darkness waded in from all horizons so that the sky contracted and there was no more light left in the world.'

I went into the church feeling nervous and found a hall with music stands and chairs. I took my tuba out of its case. Inside the church, I sat in the shadows – white gloves on – preparing to practise. That's when the bass trombone player of the Hallé found me. He was large by girth, large by nature, quick-witted and very outspoken. He took one look at my gloved hands clutching the tuba and said 'By Christ, it's fucking Al Jolson.' Off came the gloves, never to be worn again.

I played my first concert with the Hallé, as 2nd tuba in *Symphonie fantastique* at Manchester's Free Trade Hall – and all of my family came. I realised that this was most definitely for me. Barbirolli sang during the concert, which I later learnt was a quirk of his. He often sang loudly during his concerts and recordings, during the bits that he was really enjoying. Interestingly, people could get reduced-price recordings if his singing had been too intrusive.

When I started at the college, I stopped playing in brass bands, but on one occasion, I did go back to help my old band, Mirrlees. I wanted to see some of my banding mates, so I joined them for a lunchtime concert in the canteen. At the interval a shabbily dressed man who had been sweeping the floor came up to me and asked if I played with the Hallé.

'I've played with them a few times,' I said.

He told me he had been in the orchestra for ten years.

It seemed unlikely to me – I was definitely looking at the cover and not the book. 'Oh right,' I said, not for a second believing him.

I was making my excuses and stepping away when he said, 'Say hello to Sid King [who was the orchestra's 1st trumpet] when you see him. Me name's Ben Smith.' I asked one of the band who he was, but got no more than I already knew. My band mate was vague. Everyone knew the man as Ben Sweep and he turned up to clear the factory floor, and seemingly always enjoyed the music.

A few weeks later, I was rehearsing with the Hallé and saw Sid King. 'Ben Smith says hello,' I said.

Sid stopped in his tracks. 'When did you see him? He were my 2nd trumpet for ten years. One day he came to the rehearsal but then didn't turn up for the concert. He just disappeared. The orchestra tried to find him and I went around to his digs and talked to his landlady. She said that he had given her his rent, then he had gone out, saying he might be late. He never came back. I asked her if she had a forwarding address for him but she said she hadn't.'

Sad though this is, it is not unusual in this profession. In my time I have known other good players who have disappeared – often because they have a playing breakdown. Sometimes the strain gets too much and the person loses the essential self-confidence needed to perform publicly. It often happens, not at the time of a great performance, but afterwards. Perhaps it is on the Sunday afternoons of life when we are alone that we experience our crises of confidence. After witnessing a lot of players with problems, when I started teaching I did some training as a hypnotherapist, with a view to helping some of my colleagues.

THE LIVERPOOL PHILHARMONIC ORCHESTRA (THE PHIL)

I was bursting to play in another concert and fortunately I didn't have long to wait. The manager of the Liverpool Philharmonic orchestra – the Phil – had phoned the Hallé to see if their tuba player was free to do a date with them. He wasn't, but they recommended me. The Phil's tuba player was also their orchestral manager, Cliff Bevan, who was a great, all-round musician/composer/trombone player and pianist. His first job had been playing the piano with a group called the Temperance Seven, a 1920s revivalist group, complete with a vocalist who sang through a megaphone. Cliff's management work was escalating and he needed someone to do some of his tuba work, so he offered it to me. After the concert they seemed happy and I did lots more with them.

I was having a wonderful time and earning money, which was essential for my living expenses. My parents had just emigrated to Canada and they thought that as I was nineteen, I was old enough now not to need any money from them. Thinking about their own early family experiences (both my mum and my dad were in full-time work when they were fifteen) this perhaps wasn't as harsh as it now seems.

SIR JOHN

My next gig with the Hallé was to play Berlioz's *Symphonie fantastique* (again), this time in the Brangwyn Hall, Swansea, with Barbirolli. The hall was named after Swansea's most famous artist, Sir Thomas Brangwyn. He had obviously been inspired by Gauguin, and the walls of the hall were covered in paintings of semi-naked native girls, peering from behind exotic jungle flora and fruit trees. One of the orchestra's wits had described his art as 'All tits and bananas'.

It was an Indian Summer day and we sweltered through the rehearsal. Barbirolli repeatedly said that he was cold. He had put on his overcoat and scarf and had an electric heater installed on his conductor's rostrum. We sweated through the rehearsal, surrounded by incongruous jungle scenes. Barbirolli continued to mutter about being cold and that none of the orchestral players were doing what he wanted. Every few minutes he would disappear off stage for a short while, to 'warm himself up', possibly from his hip flask. Each time he came back onto the stage, he seemed to walk a little more slowly and it took him a bit longer to reach the rostrum and to get onto it. When he did, he would start to conduct, but each time a little faster. Eventually, in a flurry of waving arms, he fell backwards off the rostrum and disappeared from the orchestra's view into the stalls six feet below. In shock the orchestra stopped playing, frozen with fear. Perhaps the old man had seriously injured himself, or worse?

In the silence a slightly slurred voice floated up from the stalls. 'Don't worry my children, I am all right.'

Sir John was 'unwell', so Martin Milner, the orchestra's leader, had to conduct the concert that evening.

BEING FOUND OUT

I was loving my college life. I had met a student from the College of Art, and by my humble lights she was very sophisticated. Her last boyfriend had owned a new Saab. In comparison, I had just bought myself a second-hand bike. She said she thought that all classical musicians had limited taste. The only music she really liked was jazz. 'Well, I love jazz,' I lied.

Now at that time my only experience of music had been a few orchestral and brass band pieces. I realised that none of this would impress her, but fancying someone leads one to do strange things. Not only did I not know anything about jazz, I hadn't even heard any. By chance one evening, we ended up at the same party. We started to chat and she said 'Do you really like jazz?' her eyes brightening.

'It's my favourite music,' I lied.

'What about John Coltrane, do you like him?' she asked.

'He's my favourite jazz musician,' I said.

After the party she asked me if I would like to walk back to her flat for a coffee. It was just around the corner. I would like to be able to insert three dashes here ---, in a true Victorian novelist's tradition for a pending amorous scene, but sadly...

We arrived at her flat, which had a lot of nude pictures on the walls. She saw me looking at them. 'My self-portraits,' she said. She switched on her coffee machine and selected a record. 'Make yourself at home, I am just going to change my shoes.' The record, to my uneducated ears, sounded like a lot of high-pitched squealing noises and a fast jumble of badly played saxophone.

She reappeared smiling and looking relaxed. I pointed to the record player and said 'Excuse me, but I think you've put this record on at the wrong speed.'

The smile froze on her face, and she pointed to the door and said one word: 'Out'. I had just been introduced to John Coltrane.

I was still, (nominally) at the College, although because of Cliff's management clashes, I was doing a lot with the Phil. It was a steep learning curve for me, playing their endlessly varied repertoire, and actually getting to perform Stravinsky's *Rite of Spring*. I don't think this was the orchestra's first ever performance, but it had been many years since they had played it. We turned up to the first rehearsal; I was feeling very nervous. There was really no need; we were kindly shepherded through it by that wonderful conductor, Rafael Frühbeck de Burgos. He was a great musician who cared about the music, not about how he looked on the stand. He had no vanity and didn't belittle the players, unlike some of the maestros I was to meet later. I was reminded once again that I wanted, more than anything else, to play the tuba in a professional orchestra.

I made many musical discoveries at this time, including hearing Louis Armstrong and his band play at the Free Trade Hall.

Years later I did a recording/remake of all of Louis' earlier recordings, when the band used a tuba to play the bass line. I played in the band that accompanied his singing, which had been digitally removed from his earlier records. All of the band parts were written out by a keen fan of Louis, and Kenny Baker played all of Louis' solos. Most of these solos had been recorded and played by Louis when he was in his twenties; Kenny was over seventy when he recorded them and he played them wonderfully.

I had just started my second year at college when Cliff phoned. 'Hello Jim, it's the usual problem. Can you come to the Phil for a couple of weeks?'

I collected my dinner jacket and tuba and got the train to Liverpool. When I arrived, I went to see Cliff in his office. He said 'I've just seen your new job advertised in the paper.' He went on to explain that the Bournemouth Symphony Orchestra had a vacancy for a tuba player.

I told him I really didn't feel I was ready for a job yet, not enough experience, etc. etc. He suggested that I applied for an audition, and said he would give me a recommendation if I wanted one. He gave me their address and provided me with an envelope and notepaper. 'Do it,' he said. 'You've got nothing to lose.'

I posted the letter and two months later I was heading for Bournemouth to do an audition. This time I didn't play 'Land of my Fathers' or the Mozart horn concerto. The tuba auditions were in the afternoon, and I was one of the six applicants. Nowadays there would be at least fifty or more players applying for this position. I was the last of the six to perform. I played my prepared solo and various orchestral excerpts. When I had finished playing, the orchestra manager asked if I was free to do a trial. Because I was nineteen and I didn't know any better, I asked if anyone else was being trialled. There was an exchange of flustered glances, then the manager said, 'No there isn't'. I thought that this had to be promising for me. I successfully finished my trial and at the age of twenty I had become the tuba player with the Bournemouth Symphony Orchestra, the BSO.

I had often fantasised about confronting Mr Robert-Smythe (my old geography teacher) with the news that I would really be 'playing that tuba of mine' for a living! I'd often planned my speech. Suddenly I didn't care; revenge seemed hollow. 'May his cravat look forever grubby.' I had got what I'd always wanted.

CHAPTER 4

THE BSO AND SILVESTRI

The BSO's chief conductor was an eccentric but well-respected Romanian called Constantin Silvestri, whose direction often seemed to make little or no sense. When he asked the 1st horn player – who was playing the off-stage horn call from Wagner's *Siegfried*, while sitting in the orchestra, to play 'loud but distant', we wondered what he meant. But then there it was – a bit louder, but somehow sounding as if it was coming from a long distance.

He was often rather introspective and then the orchestra would have to suffer one of his 'brown suit days'. He would come into the rehearsal with a face like misery and we knew we were in for a day when nothing would please him. We discovered that these days seemed to coincide with him wearing a brown suit. If someone spotted him before he joined us, word would go around the players and we would adopt certain tactics for dealing with the 'brown suit day' that would certainly follow.

The rehearsal would start and within a short time Silvestri would stop conducting and say 'No' and 'Again'. We would go back to the beginning of the passage we had been playing, then start again. This whole scenario was then repeated: 'No. Again.' 'No. Again!' - without any explanation as to why we had stopped, or had to play the passage again. The braver members of the orchestra would ask what was wrong with it, only to be greeted by a doleful stare, then we would go back and play it all again.

We discovered that the only way to stop the tedium was to ask questions about the music, or to check if certain notes were correct - anything to break the monotony of the rehearsal. One day, though, nothing seemed to work. Step forth our contrabassoon player.

Now the contrabassoon can be truly melodious, or it can make an unpleasant farting sound: Handel was reputed to have said, 'Thank God it stinketh not,' when he first heard it.

Our contrabassoonist put up his hand. Silvestri put on his most doleful expression: 'Yes?'

'Maestro, would it be possible to check a note?'

'Yes?'

'Four bars after letter B, I have an F sharp, but I think some people have an F natural.'

'Play an F sharp,' said Silvestri.

A long farting noise followed. Then he said. 'Play an F natural.'

Another long farting noise followed, indistinguishable from the first. An even longer silence, then that doleful look and a shrug. 'What difference does it make?' said Silvestri.

Sadly, he died a year after I joined the orchestra, but I learned much from him about music-making. He had some eccentric ideas, but they worked really well. When we performed Tchaikovsky's *Capriccio Italien* he would insist that we played the last part at twice the speed of the tempo marking. When we did, it was a revelation. Since then, the marked tempo has always seemed too slow.

SCHOOLS' CONCERTS

During my time in the BSO I was introduced to another aspect of music-making: the 'schools' concert'.

A couple of times a year, a conductor would hire the orchestra to give a concert in the Fairfield Halls in Croydon, for the local schoolchildren.

The essential idea of an educational concert for children is a good one. Twice in one day local schools were invited to the concert hall to be introduced to some of the more accessible bits of classical music and the instruments in the orchestra. For some of them it would have been the first time they had ever heard an orchestra, and the hope was that they would enjoy the experience and perhaps even develop a passion for classical music. The conductor presenting them had been a successful violinist, and had a good knowledge of music. He was a large, florid gentleman, and seemed able enough at rehearsals. I was looking forward to finding out how these concerts would be presented.

The hall was filled with energetic chattering children, but when the concert started, the conductor seemed to go to pieces. He seemed terrified of them and went into panic mode. Red in the face and sweating he started gabbling: 'Now, Beethoven – Beethoven was going deaf. I - I - I know because I have seen his piano in Bonn and it's all worn away.'

'Now Mozart, Mozart, Mozart … He was the most kissed child in Europe … [long pause] … That makes him a genius.' If analysed, these statements sort of make sense, but the end result was a hall filled with totally mystified children and an orchestra trying inconspicuously to wipe away their tears of laughter.

MEETING MY HERO

At that time there was for me an especially good event. Alfredo Campoli, the violinist, was coming to play Mendelsohn's Violin Concerto with the orchestra. I was very excited, despite the disparaging remarks of my colleagues in the violin section. I suppose his playing had become a bit 'old-fashioned' and they referred to him rather snootily as 'the Italian ice-cream man', apparently because he scooped up the notes.

I suppose it must have been a bit of a comedown for Campoli to play his concerto in seaside venues. Twenty years earlier, he had been playing concertos with top international orchestras in the world's most prestigious concert halls. After the concert I went to see him in his dressing room, and took my LP of his Mendelssohn Violin Concerto for him to sign. He was delighted. By then, fans asking him to sign his recordings was probably becoming an infrequent occurrence. He signed my LP, then a thought seemed to occur to him. He opened his violin case and handed me his Stradivarius and bow (current value several million) and said, 'Go on, play it.' I held it briefly but quickly handed it back, terrified that I would damage it. He seemed even more delighted when I told him that I was the orchestra's tuba player.

EARLY DAYS WITH THE BSO

After Silvestri's death, George Hurst became the principal conductor of the orchestra and we continued to tour, mostly into the West Country, Plymouth, Exeter and Bristol. George was a good, able and experienced conductor, but I realised in retrospect that we didn't always appreciate his talents. He had made what was perhaps an unwise decision. He was completely bald, and he had got himself a toupee. As Spike

Milligan once said, 'A bald vain man is a hairless Greek tragedy.'

He had arrived for a rehearsal with his previous orchestra, the BBC Northern Orchestra, after a few weeks' absence from them. During this time, he had acquired his new head of hair. The orchestra had a lot of characters, including Maurice Murphy, their 1st trumpet. Wearing his full head of hair, on the dot of 10.30 George bustled into the studio, climbed onto the rostrum, opened the score, said 'Elgar' to the orchestra, and raised his baton.

Up jumped Maurice: 'Excuse me sir, but I don't think we have been introduced, would you mind telling us who you are? We can't just play for anyone you know.' Inevitable collapse of the rehearsal. The story quickly reached us in Bournemouth.

Shortly after this, George was with us conducting a 'Last Night of the Proms' concert at the Colston Hall in Bristol. Unfortunately, by accident or design, the management of the hall had a large picture of George, without his toupee, which was displayed prominently by the main entrance. At the beginning of the concert, a toupee-wearing George walked on to the platform, raised his baton, and one of the Promenaders shouted: 'Keep your hair on, George!'

My initial trial period with the orchestra had been in the early spring, and good seaside memories of my childhood were still fresh. From the age of seven to eleven, my family holidays had been in Cornwall. My dad would drive overnight from Manchester. We would set off at 6 p.m. and I would sleep in the back of the car. I would always be woken up as we went through Bristol, as my dad would always get lost there. He would ask Mum which way he should go and then ignore her suggestions. Then they would have a row. This happened every year. It seemed to be a part of their holiday ritual. I would go back to sleep again and they would wake me up at dawn, to see the sea. It was such a thrill for me to go over a hill and see the sea sparkling – the signal that our fortnight's holiday had begun.

I started my job in Bournemouth in late summer. A cellist whom I had known from college was in the orchestra, and he had found a holiday flat to share –with sea views! Winter blew in, bringing grim, grey, stormy seas and skies. The flat was poorly insulated and the only heat came from a one-bar electric heater. We were both broke, and the landlord had set the electricity meter on an extortionate tariff.

I didn't have a lot of work to do with the orchestra, so days and days were spent in the damp flat, looking at the winter weather through the condensation running down the windows. I was missing my college girlfriend, and working out if a pint in my unfriendly local pub would be cheaper than paying for the electric heater – the thing seemed to eat money. I was also missing my parents, who by then (1965) were in Canada (although I wouldn't have admitted this at the time).

The alternative entertainment was to go for a walk along the grey, stormy sea front in the pouring rain. I got jaundice and was ill for a couple of months. It wasn't a great time for me even though I was young and should have been enjoying myself.

Spring finally arrived and we moved out of the flat. My flatmate was moving in with his girlfriend and I rented half a large, unkempt house with my friend Barry, the orchestra's new 2nd oboe.

The place was unfurnished and we had lots of laughs going to furniture auctions and buying huge pieces of furniture, including a chest of drawers which stood on big carved feet.

The furniture had obviously belonged to the large, opulent old houses of the deceased gentry, which their children either didn't want, or hadn't got room for. Nobody else wanted it either, so everything was selling for a few pounds at most. I bought a huge, magnificently carved double bed for £1.50.

Life looked up after that. My oboe flatmate and I had a lot of laughs, and he became a lifelong friend. He had studied and worked in London and was anxious to return. On the odd occasions we performed there, Barry used to show me around and introduce me to some of his musician friends. In contrast, for a twenty-one year-old with little money, Bournemouth wasn't much fun.

The orchestra is good now, but back then, it was another story; it was a good place to be if you had been in the orchestra for years and were thinking about your pension, or were recently married and trying to establish yourself in a new life. The pay wasn't great, so most of the players spent all of their spare time teaching, and had little time for socialising. As I wasn't married and retirement seemed light years away, I felt that a move sooner rather than later must be a good idea.

I had done the odd concert with the LSO and the Philharmonia Orchestra by then and Barry asked if I fancied having a flat-share with him in London so we resigned from the orchestra at the same time.

While I was in the BSO, I suppose I had become a slightly nerdy collector of information about London orchestras and players. I was really pleased when an older trumpet player used to come and deputise with us. I learned that he had been in the Philharmonia Orchestra, when it was by far the most prestigious and best-paid orchestra in London. He had lots of stories of the old days and names of players that I had only ever read on my old records. He had been booked to play 3rd trumpet on our annual north of England tour, which finished with a concert in Newcastle. We finally arrived there on a wet winter afternoon. We did the rehearsal and then had time to kill until the evening concert. Most places were closed and I was walking around an outdoor market stall with him. There was a stall selling boxes of LPs. Sad and soggy, they were 50p to clear, and among them were many records by the Philharmonia Orchestra, in the days when they were 'the' recording orchestra. My friend had played on many of these recordings, which were, for me, a piece of living history.

'Look, the Mahler symphonies conducted by Furtwängler, were you playing on this?' Each time my friend would nod, but didn't say much. I wanted to know all about them; I was keen and new to the business. I was at the beginning of my career; he was at the end of his. I suppose doing a concert in a cinema, in a provincial city, and having to hang about all afternoon on a winter's day wasn't a great prospect for him.

Eventually he said, 'I will tell you about those recordings if you like. The orchestra was told that it was a great privilege for us to do them with this particular maestro and that we would be making musical history. They would win us all great fame and prestige. The maestro arrived to conduct the sessions, then he complained to the recording company and the management, saying he wasn't happy with some of the orchestra, so they were replaced, some of them permanently. He picked on two of the wind players and one of the string principals, so much, that one of them had a breakdown, and the other two resigned from the orchestra. Three players got divorced and other players turned against each other. The atmosphere was strained and unhappy, and yet while this was going on, we were being told that it was great for the orchestra, and we would realise that the sacrifice had been worth it.'

Now here we were looking at a box of those prestigious recordings that had ruined lives. 'Was it worth it? Look at that sign,' he said, pointing to the rain-smudged ink, '50p to clear! What do you think?'

CHAPTER 5

MOVING ON

My older colleagues thought my resignation a bad move, but Barry had found us a flat in London and I couldn't wait to join him.

My task now was to get rid of all the huge pieces of furniture we had bought. I tried all the local furniture shops, but only two turned up, and they both wanted me to pay them to take the stuff off my hands. By moving day, it was still there. To my shame, I took a hammer to it, then took it to the waste ground nearby and had a bonfire. It was time to move on.

My dad once told me about the time he was foreman at the Kellogg's factory after the war. It was a good place to work, especially at that time. Jobs were scarce, and as it was an American company it was more likely to be secure employment. One of his first tasks was to present an engraved retirement watch to one of the labourers. Fred had worked in the company since he was fourteen. My dad duly made his speech, saying how much the man would be missed after fifty-one years in the company, then gave him the watch. He asked him if he would like to say anything, but Fred shook his head.

My dad decided to prompt him. 'So, Fred, after fifty-one years, if you had your time again, would you still do the same thing?'

Without a moment's hesitation, Fred said, 'Oh no, not on your life, I bloody hated it.'

My dad asked him why he stayed. 'Security,' said Fred.

The story had filled me with a vague fear of being trapped.

As I sat watching the dying embers of my bonfire, it started to snow. My downstairs neighbour came out, gave me a hug, and with a very sad look she said, 'I wish I was going away,' then she went back indoors. As it got dark, I put the final item on the fire, then had a last look around. I set off for London in my old van. I had two cases, one full of books and records, the other clothes and of course, my tuba. Very little work in my diary, but this was it – I was off.

LONDON (AND WALES)

My freelance work started slowly, but I didn't mind. I was paying the rent with some part-time teaching, and had a few more gigs with the LSO, the Philharmonia Orchestra, the BBC Symphony Orchestra and quite a lot of work with the BBC Welsh Orchestra.

I used to get a lot of last-minute phone calls from the manager of the Welsh Orchestra, which didn't have a regular tuba player.

The calls usually had the same script: 'Hello Jimmy [she was the only person in the world who called me Jimmy], it's Sheila Winters here. Are you free tomorrow?'

At the start I mostly was.

'Good because I have tried everybody and I'm desperate.' I didn't mind, and though the fees for the work weren't great, the BBC, which was going through one of its egalitarian periods, paid the same generous travel and hotel expenses to all of their employees. The expenses were often more than the playing fees.

The BBC Welsh was a very small orchestra then, with two bass players, three when they performed large symphonies. Now it is the National Orchestra of Wales and it is a very good, full-size symphony orchestra. When they first launched their new name, they decided they needed a new slogan to go with it. They were doing a lot more touring around Wales, so they had their new name painted on their van. 'The National Orchestra of Wales – they are all over the place'! The new slogan was quickly replaced.

When I first started playing with them, Irwin Hoffman, an American conductor, turned up expecting a full-size symphony orchestra – sixteen first violins, fourteen seconds, twelve violas, ten cellos and eight double basses. He arrived at the studio and saw an orchestra that had six first violins, five second violins, four violas, three cellos and two double basses. He looked around and asked if the rest of the players had been wiped out by a plague.

After a pause he said, 'Though this is the first time I have seen the orchestra, it is not my first time in Cardiff, I was stationed here during the war.' Someone in the orchestra whispered 'Daddy...'

Just as I was joining the profession, the old-fashioned G bass trombone was becoming a thing of the past. It was still used in brass bands and period instrument orchestras, but nowhere else. It had a handle that was attached to the top of the slide so that the players could reach their seventh position. It was often referred to as the 'giant safety pin' (a reference to its enormous length when the slide was fully extended). It was being replaced by the larger bore B flat trombone, with a valve. This enabled bass trombone players to play their low notes without the relatively cumbersome handle.

The only player still using a G trombone in an orchestra was the bass trombone player in the BBC Welsh. It was a strange and slightly disconcerting sight to see him struggling with the long slide. He had a curious technique of keeping the slide in constant motion, which meant that all the notes slid either up or down, as he was playing them. It had a sort of glissando effect; notes would start sharp then go flat, or flat and then go sharp. As a visitor to the orchestra, it wasn't my place to comment and the rest of the brass section didn't say anything as they were counting the days to his retirement.

After a few visits I saw him as I was going into the studio, and said good morning. He looked at me and sighed, 'Oh no, not you again.'

I was a bit taken aback, so I said, 'Sorry, don't you like having me here?'

'No, I don't,' he said, '…whenever you come here, I find it impossible to play in tune'!

One of the drawbacks of being a musician is that most people think we play just because we love it. We mostly do, so we are lucky, but it often doesn't occur to people that we need to be paid for our services. On my arrival in London, I was offered a lot of duff gigs: for two hours with a worker's union protest march, I was offered a cup of tea, a sandwich and £2.50 and various bands asked if I'd jam with them 'for a laugh'. I didn't think my bank manager would find that very funny.

THE KIROV BALLET

Any anxieties about money were temporarily alleviated. I had been offered a six-week ballet season playing with the London Mozart Players at the Royal Festival Hall. The dance company was the Kirov Ballet.

They had two Russian conductors – both called Victor. One was tall, pale, thin and miserable-looking. The other was short, fat, red-faced and angry-looking. They became known to us as 'Vic Thin' and 'Vic Fat'.

We had four days to rehearse the music before the shows started. The parts had all come from the Bolshoi Ballet company and were often hand-written, and well worn. The Bolshoi players had probably played them hundreds of times, but seeing them for the first time was confusing: play two pages from this number; cut to four pages ahead; play the introduction from the beginning, etc. Finding our way around the parts was a nightmare.

Rehearsals started. Whenever anyone made a mistake, Vic Thin would stop, look miserable, then start the piece again. When Vic Fat was conducting, he would stop, go even redder and shout 'Nyet'.

Our 1st bassoon in the orchestra was Cecil James. He had recently retired from the Philharmonia Orchestra, was an excellent player and an old-school gentleman. As there were a lot of bassoon solos, he had a more difficult job finding his way around the parts than the rest of us.

Every time there was a slight slip, Vic Fat would shout 'Nyet'. After a particularly long bout of 'Nyet' directed mainly at the 1st bassoon, Cecil put his hand up. 'Excuse me, it seems evident that whatever I try to do doesn't seem to suit you. It would seem to me that we are both wasting our time here. I noticed when I left home this morning that my lawn needed mowing, so I think my time would be more advantageously spent doing that. I bid you good morning.' Cecil carefully put his bassoon into its case and calmly walked out of the rehearsal, accompanied by the sound of Vic Fat shouting 'Nyet'.

I have to say that this was a revelatory moment of my life. In my early stages of the business, I had witnessed a few conductors being unpleasant and undermining players, often leaving them with a permanent dent in their reputation and their confidence. I had often worried about how I would cope with the situation if it happened to me. Now I had witnessed the perfect way to deal with it. If the conductor didn't like it, and you didn't like it, you could walk away. As Noël Coward asks in one of his songs, 'Why must the show go on?'

PINK FLOYD AND COACH THREE

The phone rang, and an unknown voice said ''Allo, are you Jim? I run this group and someone told me you would be the one for the gig.' Here we go again, I thought, another gig for laughs, this time playing with Pink Floyd? Who they hell are they? Yes, I was the only person in the country under thirty who hadn't heard of Pink Floyd. I started to make excuses, but the fixer cut in. 'Do you want to do it? It pays £***s per day plus expenses.' The fee he mentioned was about what I usually earned for two full weeks' work. Let the good times roll.

I had a good time being one of the ten brass players playing *Atom Heart Mother* with Pink Floyd. The band members were friendly, unassuming, enthusiastic and talented. A lot of the concerts we played around Holland were in stadiums that held about 20,000 seats. The tickets sold out immediately. It began to dawn on me just how successful they were.

A couple of months later, they booked me for a series of concerts around Europe. I accepted the dates, then, as often happens, I had a clash on the last night. The BBC Symphony Orchestra had asked me to do some concerts around Europe with them. All of their dates fitted around the Floyd's dates except for the last concert, when they both had concerts in Hamburg, on the same night. I told the orchestra that it might be difficult for me to do their work, but I would let them know. I talked to the band, and they asked what time the BBC Symphony concert in Hamburg would finish. I said 9.45. They suggested I get a cab to their gig as soon as I had finished my concert with the orchestra. When you are freelancing, there is nothing more satisfying than 'fitting them in'.

The day before the concert, I flew to Hamburg in the morning and checked into the Hotel Intercontinental where the BBC orchestra had reservations. It was a newly opened hotel, in fact it was the hotel's very first day and they obviously wanted to make a very good impression. Everything was bright and shiny and the hotel staff were immaculately clad in their new matching uniforms.

I sat in the lobby, waiting for the orchestra to arrive. I was feeling decidedly underdressed, as most of the other guests seemed to be smartly suited business people. The waiters fussed around straightening the magazines on the coffee tables and each other's bow ties. They gazed at me a bit reproachfully, obviously feeling that I was making their lobby look a bit untidy.

The BBC had played a concert in Amsterdam the previous day. They were now due to arrive by coach and have the rest of their day free. Their journey had been scheduled to last for three hours, but there had obviously been a long delay, and it wasn't until five hours later that the first coach arrived.

The people in the orchestra who got on the first and second coaches were usually the readers and the quieter members, sometimes referred to by the ruder brass players as 'pond life'. They got out of their coach and filed past a full-size stagecoach in the hotel grounds, which was advertising a forthcoming event, and came into the lobby. The hotel staff sprang into action to help the musicians with their shabby suitcases. The second coach arrived, with much the same result, and then coach three arrived. As they had had a much longer journey than had been predicted, and as it was their free day, they had begun to celebrate early.

The players started to disembark. One of the principal cellists was wearing a piece of cardboard over his face and was being guided by his friend, a wacky Irish bass player. The hair of one of the trombonists had fallen over his face and he was gnashing his teeth and muttering darkly in Polish. Two members of the brass section were laughing and dancing around the lawn and falling over. Then they noticed the stagecoach.

They couldn't resist it, they all climbed into it, taking their carrier bags of refreshments with them and closing the door. I was thoroughly enjoying watching this impromptu pantomime from the hotel. The outraged mutterings of the staff were growing. The manager of the hotel marched forth and attempted to get the door of the stagecoach open, but it was being held shut. Suddenly it was released and as the door flew open the manager fell backwards on to the lawn. Wiping himself down, he began to mount the steps of the coach, when hands, some of them bearing bottles of alcohol, beckoned him to join them. He turned and fled back into the hotel. The rest of the day was spent with a lot of the orchestra 'resting'.

As I didn't need a rest I went for a wander around Hamburg and eventually ended up back at the hotel for afternoon tea. That's when I spotted Placido Domingo, the tenor, and a man in a white jacket approaching the piano. Placido wasn't so well known in England at the time, but I had been lucky enough to play with the LSO when they recorded *Aida* with him as Radames. The whole orchestra had been really impressed and I was looking forward to hearing him sing again. I assumed that the man in the white coat was going to accompany him, but

Domingo sat down on the piano stool, while the other man stood by the piano. With a grin Placido started to play some Schubert – *Winterreise*, I think. The man in the white coat started to sing (rather badly). It turned out he was a waiter at the hotel and a friend. He had asked Placido to play the piano for him.

The next day we did our performance of *The Rite of Spring*. On a high at the end of the show, still in my tails, I carried my tuba into a waiting taxi which drove across Hamburg to the Pink Floyd concert. I got a cheer as I went onto the stage; the audience obviously thought my white tie and tails looked the part. As the band had promised, they had waited for me and started the piece just after I sat down.

Afterwards, I changed out of my tails back at the hotel and went to meet the orchestra for a drink. The bar where we met seemed more like a seedy nightclub. Some of the orchestra had been there for a while. I bought a round of drinks and was treated to the sight of one of the orchestra's brass players lying face down on the stage, happily smiling and naked except for his underpants, which he was wearing on his head. He was trying to dissuade a naked stripper from inserting a candle between the cheeks of his buttocks. It had been a very long and bizarre couple of days.

When I got home from the tour, John Amis (Kingsley's brother), who was doing some freelance work for the BBC, interviewed me for Radio 3. It was a rather dull interview and I couldn't help feeling that it would have been a lot more interesting if I had been able to tell him about the stagecoach, Domingo's accompanying and the nightclub.

Who knows, it might have given the station's listeners a bit of a shock.

TUBAS IN THE PIAZZA

After the fruit market had been moved away from Covent Garden there was a complete re-build of the area. It was to be called the Piazza and I hadn't yet seen it. It was approaching Christmas when an ex-tuba student of mine phoned. He was organising a mass 'tuba ensemble', playing Christmas carols for charity. We would play in the Piazza, would I join them? He planned to begin the playing at 3 p.m. It seemed like a good thing to do so I agreed.

I was a little late when I got off the tube with my tuba at Covent Garden station. As I wasn't quite sure where the Piazza was, I started to walk towards the Opera House, then stopped and listened. I was aware of a sort of low rumbling sound, which seemed to have the odd suggestion of a tune. The sound got louder and I was eventually greeted by the sight of about fifty tubas of all shapes and sizes, mainly large ones, playing 'Silent Night'. The sight looked like a Monty Python sketch, but with the jokes replaced by the sound of low dole-full mass tuba vibrations.

I joined them and we began to play the next carol: 'We Wish You a Merry Christmas' and a Happy New Year'. A noisy group of youths appeared, each carrying a can of strong lager. Here was the perfect opportunity for them to have something to jeer about. They stood in front of us shouting insults, but within a few minutes they slowly fell silent. The rest of our audience should have been cheered by it, but it seemed to have the opposite effect. The air seemed to thicken around us as we played, like some presage of a minor dementor visitation. After they had listened to us, they walked slowly away, looking wiser but sadder.

'We Wish You An Unhappy Christmas and a Prosaic New Year'! As dusk started to fall, everyone silently drifted away.

If you are still with me, readers, as you must have realised by now, freelancing can be very varied. I would now like to recall three events of which I am not proud, and three events of which I am.

CHAPTER 6

THREE OF MY NOT-SO-PROUD MOMENTS

1 'PADSTOW LIFEBOAT'

We were playing a concert of some of Sir Malcom Arnold's music for his 80th-birthday celebrations. At the end of the concert, he was to be given a standing ovation, then invited on to the stage to be presented with an award. Our 1st trumpet player had an idea and suggested that as he was being handed this award, the brass section in the orchestra could play the 'Padstow Lifeboat', a march Malcom had written for his local brass band in Cornwall. This seemed like a good idea, so the music was handed to the brass players; we planned just to play the first part.

We finished the last piece in the concert, his 5th Symphony, but immediately the applause started, Malcom walked straight on to the platform, stood on the rostrum, picked up the score of the 5th Symphony, opened it at the beginning and started to conduct it. Now he had always been keen on celebrations, and as it was his 80th birthday he had probably spent the day doing quite a lot of celebrating. Our conductor froze, and the 1st trumpet said 'Quick lads. "Padstow Lifeboat".' We began to play it and Arnold put down his score of the symphony and began conducting his march with great enthusiasm. The audience started to clap in time. It seemed as though the situation was saved, until we reached the end of the first part of the march. His conducting became even more vigorous and some of the band took the repeat sign back to the beginning and some of us carried on playing the next part of the march. Clashing discords followed and one by one we stopped playing. We were left with the sounds of the embarrassed coughing of the audience and orchestra, some sporadic applause and the singing of the birthday boy still energetically conducting his march.

2 BRASS QUINTET FIASCO

I had been a member of a brass quintet for a couple of years. We did concerts in different venues and we all enjoyed playing new repertoire. We were to play a concert in Bournemouth's Royal Bath Hotel. About a week before the gig our 1st trumpet fell ill so we replaced him with a player we knew. He didn't know the last piece that we were going to play in the concert, which was a complex modern one, but we did manage to do a couple of short rehearsals. He was sure it wouldn't be a problem and said he would try and find time to look at the piece. He was always very confident and he reassured us that it would be fine. We were playing in the ballroom of the hotel, which was set out so the elderly residents could have tea and cake during the concert.

When we went on to the stage and started to play, the sound of conversation, clinking of plates and tea cups and the high-pitched whistling of hearing aids hardly disturbed us at all! We realised with relief that it wasn't exactly going to be a high-pressure gig.

Months before, the tuba player in the Bournemouth Orchestra and myself had applied for a particular piece of work. It had been given to me and he was very cross about it, feeling that he was a better player and that the appointment had been fixed. From the things I heard he had said, it seemed that he was still resentful. I half-dreaded seeing him at the concert and I was relieved when he didn't turn up.

The concert was going fine, and our deputy 1st trumpet was doing a good job. We got to the final movement of the last piece and we were beginning to relax (always a mistake). Suddenly our guest trumpet player got lost. He had a few tries to find his place, then gave up. There is a well-known syndrome in music called the domino effect – one player makes a mistake and other players follow. The horn player started to wobble with nerves and the trombone player also got the shakes and stopped playing.

A back door banged open and 'that' tuba player crashed into the room. At this point there were only two players actually playing: the 2nd trumpet player and me. Now I would have thought that the only reason the tuba player would turn up would be in the hope that he could witness my disappointing playing. His prayers were answered in spades. As we got to the last bars of the piece, I played my final solo and completely cocked it up. Everything crashed into a shocked silence. Even the mumbled conversations had stopped. The only sounds that could be heard were the whistling of hearing aids and the loud delighted laughter of the tuba player as he walked away down an echoing corridor. I think I had more than made his day.

3 ONE DOOR CLOSES... FROM HERO TO ZERO

I worked for lots of fixers. The best-paid gigs were jingles – doing music for TV/film adverts. Usually a one-hour jingle session paid the same as a three-hour film session. A fixer I didn't know phoned and booked me for a double jingle (a two-hour session) in a tiny studio in Soho. I turned up to discover that I was the only player there.

The situation was explained to me. A Swiss insurance company had made a film about a mole and they wanted about 15 seconds of music and sounds to accompany the film, which they showed to me. A cartoon mole was happily burrowing along just below the surface of a lawn; then it collided with a spade, which had been sunk into the lawn. The caption appeared, 'You never know when you may need insurance'. They had decided they wanted the film to be accompanied by a tuba, but they hadn't written any music. Could I just watch the film a couple of times more and do something 'appropriate'? I watched the film, and made up a silly sort of tune with some sound effects. When I played it, the people in the recording booth loved it and said it was perfect. They seemed completely happy and paid me for a two-hour session which had lasted about fifteen minutes. I left feeling well pleased.

Three months later I got another call from the same fixer, to go back to the same studio to do a one-hour jingle. Remembering how pleased they were with my last efforts, I duly arrived for the session, thinking the whole thing wouldn't take long. However, instead of the initial three people who had been in the box, there were now seven. It turned out that they still had the piece of film they had made, but had lost the soundtrack that I had done. Could I just play the identical version I had played last time?

I had made the first one up on the spur of the moment three months before and I had completely forgotten what I had done. I looked at the mole film again and made something up. The seven people in the box listened to it, then they had a lengthy discussion. I was told it wasn't really quite what they wanted. The previous version had been perfect, why couldn't I do the same thing again? I had played a lot of music in the interim and I really couldn't remember what I had done originally.

I spent a fruitless hour making up endless tunes and doing sound effects, but I felt that nothing would compare in their minds to the original, especially as it was now being discussed by seven 'experts'. With lots of sad shakings of heads, I finally finished the session and left. I thought of one of the grimmer sayings of the freelance musician: one door closes, and another one slams in your face.

THREE OF THE THINGS I AM PROUD OF (BLOWING MY OWN TUBA)

1 SHOWBOAT: ABBEY ROAD AND THE LONDON SINFONIETTA

John McGlinn had spent many years researching the original music and scripts for Jerome Kern's *Showboat*. He had reinstated a lot of the score that had been deleted in the past, and had assembled a wonderful cast of singers: Frederica von Stade was to play Magnolia, with an all-star line-up. John McGlinn was also conducting.

The tuba part was a traditional bass part, straightforward, perfectly scored and lovely to play. It was pleasure to turn up to work every day and enjoy the playing and wonderful singing. When the recording was released, it was reviewed on Radio 3. One of the reviewers said: 'How nice to hear such a good bass line played so well on the tuba.' I never found out his name, but thank you, whoever you are.

2 'SAN"

Simon Rattle wanted to record at Abbey Road with the London Sinfonietta. He arrived to do the first rehearsal with his usual enthusiasm and imagination. He planned to do a mixture of the original orchestrations of Gershwin's *Rhapsody in Blue* and many more pieces from the twenties. He had planned to call the CD *The Jazz Album*. I thought that the tuba part would be a traditional oompah bass line, which it mostly was, but I was in for a surprise.

One of the pieces was called 'San'. Simon wanted me to play the lower saxophone solo on the tuba. Usually, the saxophone has lot of solos to play, unlike the tuba. I said I would give it a go and I played it. Simon liked it and he asked me to play the solo each time. Later we did a Promenade concert and I played it. The Promenaders went mad, and I appreciated their enthusiasm. I got a bow; it was nice to be a soloist for a change.

3 JABBA THE HUTT

I was booked to do two sessions with the National Philharmonic Orchestra at Kingsway Hall. The recording was music from *Star Wars* and it had a mixture of John Williams's music from all of the three (at that time) *Star Wars* films. I turned up to the session early so I could have a look at 'the dots' – and it was just as well that I did. Looking through the pad of tuba music, I saw a piece titled 'Jabba the Hutt'. In brackets was written 'tuba solo – three minutes, 37 seconds'. There were two pages of complex music: apparently the solo had been cut from the original scene in the film as it had got in the way of the dialogue. I was still having a first look at it, when the conductor Charles (Chuck) Gerhardt suggested I played while I had a fresh lip because it was a high and tiring blow. The red light went on; I played. After three minutes and 37 seconds the light went off, and a huge cheer went up from the whole orchestra. I asked if they wanted to do another recording for safety. But Chuck had already moved on: 'Thanks tuba, that was great; next number please everyone.'

CHAPTER 7

SNAPE AND BRITTEN

Mansell, the manager of the English Chamber Orchestra (ECO) phoned me. 'Could you get down to Snape Maltings as soon as possible? Ben [Britten] is conducting and we need a tuba player.' When I arrived, the rehearsal had already started, and I went on to the stage as discreetly as possible. Britten looked up: 'Ah tuba, good.' The ECO was playing his Cello Symphony, which he had written for Rostropovich, who was playing the solo cello part. Whenever I played, Rostropovich would look around at me and shout, 'MGM.'

'What does he mean?' I asked the trombonist next to me.

'I haven't the faintest idea,' he said. Rostropovich kept repeating, 'MGM, MGM.' I tried to smile as though I knew what he meant.

Britten finally explained. 'Ah, tuba, what Slava [Rostropovich] wants, is for you to make a sound like the lion on the MGM film titles – in other words, "roar".'

This was the first of my many visits to Snape and getting to know Britten's music and this wonderful part of Suffolk where Britten and his partner Peter Pears had made their home. Initially I found his music a bit inaccessible but the more familiar I became with the countryside, the more I understood his music.

Behind the Maltings is a lovely walk to Iken Church, through the tall sighing reeds. If you stop and listen for a while, you hear, almost subliminally, the music somehow coming through the air and out of the marshes. You imagine the storms at sea, from the opera *Peter Grimes*; the space and the sky; a procession of children with animal masks tripping along the path, cheerfully singing the 'Kyrie' from his children's oratorio, *Noye's Fludde*; and the haunting distant horn calls from his *Serenade for Tenor, Horn and Strings*, where you can make out the 'horns of elf-land gently blowing'.

I have played his last work, the opera *Death in Venice*, many times, and the more harrowing passages still deeply disturb me. Britten died many years ago; his music, for those who get to know it, will last for many lives into the future.

TEACHING AT THE GUILDHALL SCHOOL OF MUSIC

I started teaching at the Guildhall School of Music two years after I came to London, in 1974. Initially I was asked if I would be willing to share the job with John Fletcher, their tuba professor. John would phone on a regular basis and ask if I could do the next two or three weeks for him. After two terms he asked me to take over all his classes, saying that though he was happy to do the odd group class, he didn't really have the time to teach regularly; so I became a tuba professor.

I spent thirty years teaching at the GSM. For the first ten years I taught alone before being joined by a well-qualified teacher, Patrick Harrild. I was lucky enough to have a lot of fine students, many of whom are now good friends and successful musicians. Plenty of them have since thanked me for encouraging them to go into the parts of the music world that don't solely rely on playing. Many have great jobs in management and music administration. I am very proud of all of them.

There are more applicants each year for all the good music colleges, but sadly there are fewer playing opportunities. The days when there were few applicants for jobs have long gone. The last vacancy for the LSO tuba job received more than two hundred applications.

Apologies for being discouraging, but the only reason anyone would apply for a place in music college is if you feel you have to do music more than anything else in the world, and if you didn't, you would spend the rest of your life regretting not having given it your best shot. When I was interviewing applicants, it was always essential to me to ascertain that they had a total commitment. I did sometimes find that their parents wanted them to get a place, because they had failed to get a place themselves when they applied years before. As parents we all have to learn not to live vicariously through our children. If you simply have to try for yourself and you do succeed, you will have a great, if not very well-paid, life being somehow involved in music.

Over my long professional life, I have seen a lot of players have performance breakdowns, sometimes permanently. This often happens when players have trouble with a small part of the music, perhaps with a piece that they've played easily many times. It is very distressing to see a colleague who is a very good player struggling with something you may have heard them play brilliantly many times before. Some players give up playing altogether.

I had a postgraduate student who wanted to spend a year with me at the Guildhall. He was aware of how competitive finding a job would be, so I accepted him. I suggested he played to the other students, which we all did regularly. He was in a terrible state. In our lesson later, he explained that while he could play for strangers, playing in front of people he knew made him very nervous. This had been happening at his last college and he seemed to think it was getting worse. We talked a lot about it and I took him to see a hypnotherapist I'd heard of, who helped him overcome his nerves. I was so impressed that I took a three-month training course with this hypnotherapist so I could help other students. I am now convinced that difficulties that manifest themselves as physical problems can often be caused by mental ones. A good hypnotherapist can often help redress some mental issues which can lead to the alleviation of physical symptoms. One of my students now practises hypnotherapy for a living.

THE TUBA AND A SENSE OF HUMOUR

An important aspect of being a tuba player is having a sense of humour. People will be anxious to tell you a joke, often the same one. It involves someone mistaking the tuba for a gold-plated toilet.

I was doing a run of Wagner operas with ENO, English National Opera. The orchestra was in the middle of Wagner's *Ring* cycle (four operas, each one more than four hours long). I was thinking about the opera as I was approaching the Stage Door, my thoughts already in the involving world of late Wagner operas. I was spotted by a man who noticed that I was carrying my tuba. He pointed to it and said 'Playing your Oompah, eh?'

THE LSO IN THE USA

I was getting a lot of extra work with the LSO because their marvellous tuba player, John Fletcher, was also a member of the Philip Jones Brass Ensemble (PJBE), and as he was often obliged to do their work, I was asked if I would cover for him.

André Previn was the LSO's newly appointed conductor. This was before he had appeared on the *Morecambe and Wise* Christmas show. Some of the orchestra members felt rather snobbishly that he was more of a pop conductor, but he had been a great Hollywood film conductor, composer, arranger, jazz pianist, and was married at the time to the actress Mia Farrow – in short, he was great box-office material. He was due to conduct the LSO for a three-week tour down the Eastern Seaboard, from New York to Miami and I accepted the booking with enthusiasm.

The first concert was in New York and I fell instantly in love with the city and its attractions. At the Carnegie Deli, I held back from their famous salt beef on rye – what seemed like half a kilo of beef, topped with gherkins and a thin slice of rye bread. I asked for an omelette instead. 'What kind of a goddam order is that,' snapped the waiter. 'Do you want ham, cheese, the deli omelette?'

I thought for a moment, then said, 'Oh sorry, may I have a cheese omelette?'

'A cheese omelette, right?'

'Yes, thank you.'

'Thank *you*,' he replied. 'You must be English.' He rolled his eyes.

Years later, when Sting released 'An Englishman in New York', I couldn't help being reminded of my first time in the Big Apple.

We played our concert that night in the Carnegie Hall, then went for a drink in the Carnegie Tavern. While I was at the bar, Bill, one of the orchestra's members, came to join me. I asked if he wanted a drink but he was too distracted to answer. He was picking at his thumbs and bouncing up and down on the balls of his feet. I knew this was what we had all seen on lots of David Attenborough's nature programmes – the beginning of Bill's mating ritual. His eyes were fixed on a very well-dressed young woman who had just come into the bar. I could hear Attenborough's voice in my head: 'Inexorably the bull of the herd approached the female!'

He told her he had been playing in the concert, asked her if she had enjoyed it, and if he could he buy her a drink – his usual patter. She said that she hadn't been at the concert, but yes, he could buy her a drink. After they had chatted for a few minutes, they left, with Bill giving us a wink. About twenty minutes later, a very dishevelled Bill – his carefully combed hair all over the place – burst into the bar and ordered a large brandy, and fast. He said the woman had invited him back to her apartment, and then mentioned that there was a minimum charge of $150. He'd replied that he would show her a good time for nothing, before trying to kiss her. At which point, she pulled a knife on him. When we asked him what had happened next, he thought for a minute, then said, 'Well, then I suppose all the romance went out of it.' According to many authors, people who lead rich emotional lives are often a bit slow on the uptake.

We would all often laugh at Bill's antics, but for many years he was often surprisingly successful with the ladies. His obvious approach seemed initially to slightly offend, then they seemed to fall for his charms. His total lack of self- doubt was impressive in a way. As he got older, he met women who often got a bit cross with him. I watched him doing his chat-up lines and being a bit too insistent with one woman. Eventually in exasperation she said to him 'F*** off Grandad'. Undeterred, he re-joined our group, telling us that he was sure the woman must have been a lesbian.

The following evening, we were having a drink on my balcony when we saw a man standing on the balcony opposite. He was naked from the waist down, and was masturbating onto the pedestrians on the street below. 'Look at that filthy bastard,' someone said and we all shared in the general outrage. One member of our party didn't comment. He was one of the few genuinely good people ever, and he had never been known to say anything unkind about anyone.

'What do you think of that, Arthur?' we asked.

He was quiet for a while, then looked up at the sunny sky and said, 'Well, he's picked a nice evening for it.'

Our concert tour moved south down the Eastern Seaboard. We did a concert in a small, scruffy one-horse town. It had taken a few hours of winding through the mountain roads by coach to get there. The concert was in a sort of community gymnasium, surrounded by a lot of dodgy bars, and many of the residents were openly wearing guns.

It really didn't seem like the sort of place that would welcome an orchestral concert. There was hardly enough room on the makeshift stage for the orchestra and by the time we had managed to sit down we were wondering why we'd bothered. While we were waiting for Previn to come on, three workmen came on dragging a huge rostrum in front of the orchestra. Now we can start, we thought. Then the Mayor came in, stood on the rostrum and began a speech welcoming the 'Boston Symphony Orchestra'. We were fuming. After fifteen minutes the rostrum was dragged off the stage. Then Previn came on. He took one look at the orchestra, realised the situation, turned to the audience and said, 'Ladies and gentlemen, I was going to give you the next five years' schedule for the LSO. But I guess now we haven't time...' With all tension diffused, he turned to the orchestra and smiled.

We gave them a good concert.

From there we moved on to Charlottesville, which was a huge college campus next to a small town. After the concert, we had a drink in one of the bars. No sign of Bill. Someone said he had met three brass students, female of course, and had invited them back to his hotel for a drink. A little later as we were walking up the drive back towards the hotel, three young women came running down, screaming with laughter. Bill was leaning out of the window of his hotel room shouting after them, 'Well, it's your loss.' If God loves a trier, then Bill would be at the top of his Christmas card list.

We next headed down the coast for a week in Florida. This was going to be the easy bit of the tour. We only had to perform a few concerts and the orchestra had always had a good welcome every time they had played there.

At that time the LSO didn't have any women members, which rightly caused indignation. After our first concert, Previn did a TV interview, hosted by one of the channel's leading lady presenters. The inevitable question was asked: 'Mr Previn, why are there no women members in the LSO?'

He was often asked this question and realising that it was probably going to be repeated many more times he said, 'On the contrary, we have six women in the LSO.' The next day an outraged article appeared in the *Daytona News Journal*, stating: 'Not only does Andre Previn have six women in the LSO, but he makes them all dress up as men.' I imagine the journalist had spent the evening, during the concert, looking at all of us dressed in tails and trying to decide which of us were really women.

I was sad when the tour finished and I was back to doing ...

MORE SCHOOL CONCERTS

I was asked to deputise with a brass quintet. Two weeks of playing three or four concerts a day in different schools. The quintet was clearly very practised at presenting these and the leader explained the format: we'd play some tunes, talk a bit about the music, then show the children each of the instruments starting with the smallest – the trumpet, then the horn, the trombone, then the tuba. Each player would play a tune: mine was 'The Elephant', from Saint-Saëns's *Carnival of the Animals*.

Each time I played the children were asked to guess which animal I was trying to show. The hands would shoot up; 'An elephant,' they answered in unison. By the end of the first week, I was getting tired of playing 'The Elephant' and I wondered what would happen if I played a different tune. I chose 'The Swan' cello solo, also from *Carnival of the Animals*, then Zoroastro's aria from *The Magic Flute*, and finally Mendelssohn's 'Oh for the Wings of a Dove'. Whatever I played, the children always said 'Elephant' and I couldn't figure out why. Then I got my answer. Whenever I played, the other four players stood behind me with their left hands on their hips to represent an elephant's ear and their right arms straight out and waving like trunks.

At the end of one day's concerts, we got to our final school. I played a bit of the slow movement of the Haydn trumpet concerto, and the players all stood behind me doing their mime. The kids were asked to name the animal. A little girl shot her hand up.

'Yes?'

'A teapot,' she said.

CHAPTER 8

TOURING OPERA

'The conductor wants to see the trombone section in his room immediately,' we were told by the orchestra manager.

We were doing our penultimate week of a seven-week opera tour and we had arrived at our penultimate week's venue to play a Verdi opera.

The young conductor sadly wasn't very good, but was very full of his own importance. Every day we were seeing him miscue the players and singers, hearing his snide remarks, and experiencing his general ineptitude. The fact that he sweated over the orchestra's front-desk players in close proximity to him had led the principal viola to christen him 'Flailing Pork'. He had lost the respect of all the performers within the first two weeks of the tour.

The three trombone players were good friends of mine, and they spent a lot of time in the local hostelries. There was a wonderful one near the theatre, which sold lovely beer out of wooden barrels. I had joined them for a lunchtime pint, then reluctantly left them to it. I had bought a new and rather expensive instrument (a cimbasso) and it was very different to any of my previous tubas. Determined to make a good job of playing it, I was limiting myself to enjoying one drink after the shows were finished.

The trombone players arrived minutes before the evening show started. Judging by the gales of laughter and the cloud of fumes that accompanied them into the pit, they had clearly been having a good time. Every time anyone made a mistake, there was lots of shuffling and giggling. Just after the opera came to an end the orchestra manager came into the pit and summoned the trombones as instructed. He told me that I need not go with them. I explained that, as I was a member of the section, I would be going with them. When we arrived at the conductor's room, he informed us, in his most important loud voice, that this '…just wasn't good enough' and that 'the drinking would have to stop forthwith'.

I looked at my colleagues. P., the 1st trombone, was leaning rather unsteadily on a table, looking glazed. R., the 2nd trombone, was standing bolt upright, nodding at everything that was being said, but he seemed a bit reluctant to actually attempt any form of speech. I thought that maybe the conductor did have a point.

M., the bass trombone, hadn't said anything; he was notorious for being able to drink very large amounts of alcohol without this having any effect on his ability to speak or play perfectly. He was said to have 'hollow legs'. Colleagues who had spent time drinking with him before shows often regretted the fact that he was always fine for the concert, while only too often they were not.

M. began speaking to the conductor in what sounded to me like a stream of Dickensian legalese. 'Excuse me, but am I to understand that you are making intimations of inebriation at this juncture?'

The conductor said, 'Well yes, I am afraid so…'

M. silenced him with a gesture. 'If that is the case, I, for one, will have no recourse other than to tender my resignation forthwith.' R., standing upright, nodded his agreement while P. was still slumped against the table.

The conductor started to look a bit panicky – he suddenly realised that he might lose his whole trombone section before the run ended. 'No, please gentlemen, perhaps I spoke a little too hastily,' he said.

M. spoke again. 'I think under the circumstances you leave us no alternative action except that of resignations.'

By now the conductor was looking positively scared. He went down on his hands and knees. 'No, please gentlemen, I beg you, don't resign; in fact, I would like to take you all to the pub and buy you a large drink!'

Trying to turn my tears of laughter into a cough, I fled from the room.

THE BBC AND BOULEZ

The BBC Symphony Orchestra's tuba job became vacant and I decided I would audition for it. This time there were nearly seventy applicants and I did my first audition at 9.30 in the evening. I had been offered two commercial recording sessions during that day with another orchestra. I could either spend the day practising for the audition, or hope that there wasn't too much for me to play in the sessions.

I decided to do the sessions, but they were a really big blow for all of the brass and when I turned up for the audition in the evening, I had a very tired lip. It was all going fine until Boulez (the conductor) asked me to play a high tuba solo from *Pictures at an Exhibition*, composed by Mussorgsky and orchestrated by Ravel. The solo is always played by tenor tuba (euphonium) but Boulez said he wanted to hear it played on the bass tuba as it was written in the tuba part.

I attempted it but my lip wasn't up to it, and I split a couple of the high notes. As I was leaving the audition the orchestra manager followed me out and said that Boulez wanted to hear me again. I turned up for the next audition at 9 a.m. the following week. I had a good lip and the solo was fine. I was given a short trial and then I was offered the job. I did deliberate about taking it – after all, my freelancing seemed successful. But at this time, I had an experience that was to permanently change my life.

I suppose that I had always had a problem forming permanent relationships. They would start happily enough but within a short time, I would start to feel a bit trapped and we would drift apart. At that time I had been in a new relationship for a few months and I felt that it wasn't going anywhere. Then the bombshell. She announced that she was pregnant – had forgotten to take her contraceptive pill. I realised that I couldn't possibly leave her and a child.

Six months later our son was born. As I gazed into his young-old face, he looked wise and new, and he reminded me of my father in some ways. A few lines that I had always thought of as a piece of doggerel came into my mind: 'The child is the father of the man'. To me these words became real. I needed to look after this wonderful child, maybe children so I accepted the BBC job. A close friend of mine said, 'Well let's face it, this is something you've wanted for years.' I protested, but the more I thought about it, the more I realised that he was right.

I watched my son and two years later my daughter grow, with pride and joy – still do. My partner and I got married and spent fifteen years together, not unhappily, before going our separate ways.

Pierre Boulez was the BBC's highly rated chief conductor and he was a stickler for correct notes and tuning. Some of the players had nicknamed him 'The French Correction'. He had remarkably attuned ears and amid a fantastic cacophony of sound, he would stop the rehearsal and tell the 2nd flute that his third quaver in bar 35 should be a C sharp - and he'd be right.

It was part of the BBC Orchestra's remit to play new compositions, so we were always working on something new. Some of the more traditional players resented this. I wasn't too keen either, but I figured that if it had been written, then it deserved a performance, and it had to be played as well as possible, even if the piece contained strange and disturbing noises. Only time would tell if it was any good. After all a lot of the pieces written in the past might rightly or wrongly have been confined to life's dustbin at or soon after the time of their creation. Just to take one example, we all know Dvorak's cello concerto, violin concerto, wonderful symphonies, and so on. Do we know his piano concerto? I have only played it once and it became apparent why it was seldom performed – it wasn't really anything like as good as the rest of his compositions.

Boulez seemed to be very serious and exacting, but underneath this façade lay a terrific sense of humour. David Theodore, the principal oboe of the orchestra, told me about an audition that he, some of the wind principals and Boulez had held for the 2nd oboe position. The co-principal oboe player, Robin – who resembled David physically – wasn't present at this audition. David had a scrupulously fair, if sometimes lengthy, method of auditioning. You generally know after just a few bars if the player is the one that you are looking for, but David always gave each candidate a long time to settle themselves, perhaps hoping that, by the end of the audition, they would have realised that they didn't reach the required standard.

A very confident candidate, let's call him Mr X, arrived. He launched himself into the set solo piece before bodging his way through the orchestral excerpts. His tone was awful, reminiscent of an Indian snake charmer. Finally – and mercifully – the audition ended. Mr X, highly pleased with himself, beamed at them all and asked if they wanted anything else.

David held the door open for him and he looked into David's eyes, smiled and said 'Robin, thank you, I really enjoyed that.'

As the door closed Boulez said, 'And that was the final nail in his coffin.'

We were on tour in Europe and the last piece in the concert was Stravinsky's *Firebird*. Boulez was conducting. We had just got to the penultimate movement, 'Kastchei's Dance'. This evil giant has a snarling two-note motif, which is handed on throughout the orchestra. The tuba is the first to play and I was counting like mad. I had played the piece many times and I came in with great confidence – four bars early! The 1st trombone, who was supposed to play next, nearly dropped his instrument with shock. The music rocked for a second then righted itself.

At the end of the concert, I went to Boulez's dressing room to apologise for my blunder. I knocked on his door, which was opened by Boulez, who was tucking into an enormous box of chocolates. I began my apologies. He stopped me, laughed, handed me the box, and said, 'Never mind – have a chocolate.' This was to become a catchphrase whenever any player made an obvious mistake.

The tour continued around Germany, with our penultimate concert in Munich and our last concert in Rotterdam. At the end of our rehearsal of Bruckner's 4th Symphony, an American came up and introduced himself to us. He told us he was the principal 'hornist' of the Munich Philharmonic Orchestra, and much else besides, practically down to what he had for tea and the colour of his socks.

As we inched away from him, he told us he was going to come to our concert that evening, to see what sort of job our 1st horn would make of the Bruckner symphony. The fact that he didn't have a ticket for the sold-out concert didn't worry him. 'I can always get in,' he said, before asking what we would be wearing. Just before the concert he turned up in his white tie and tails, with his French horn, which he left in the Munich Philharmonic's band room – the same room that we were using for our instruments. He found a seat near the front of the hall, and fixed his eyes on our 1st horn – Alan Civil – who played beautifully throughout. After the concert he followed us to a bar, and continued talking about himself. Finally, he left, but dashed back a few minutes later in a panic. His horn had been locked in the hall. Peter, a member of our horn section, had told him that as we were playing in Rotterdam the following day, the orchestra's porters had probably collected the instruments from the band room, loaded up their truck and might even be en-route to Rotterdam already. He ran out of the bar, and Peter started to laugh, explaining that though the porters had loaded up the truck they were probably staying the night in a local hotel, but the man hadn't given him the chance to tell him. We did feel rather sorry for him and had a look at possible hotels the porters might have used, but failed to find them, and returned to the bar.

BAD BEHAVIOUR

The only tour that the BBC did at that time was an annual three-week one, nearly always around Europe. It was the only time, apart from the busy two-month Proms schedule, that the orchestra ever really worked outside the studio in Maida Vale.

The tour did seem to provide a sense of release for a lot of the orchestra and so the behaviour was sometimes over the top. We were just nearing the end of one of these tours, and most of the travelling had been done on buses, which often involved early starts after late-night concerts.

After a desultory breakfast the orchestra, especially Coach Three, would get on the bus accompanied by the odd grumble but mostly in silence, and we would head for another autobahn. Connor, one of our livelier Irish bass players, would always insist on setting his alarm clock. When it went off, it was the signal that the sun was 'over the yard arm' (time for a drink). After what often seemed like an interminably long time, Connor's alarm clock would ring and with a few cheers, bottles would be opened.

There had been a lot of lively behaviour on this particular tour and Charles, the orchestra manager, was finding it all a bit wearing. He was an extremely nice man, but not particularly organised. The orchestra arrived at La Fenice Theatre in Venice to find that the theatre was locked. The hall's management denied knowing anything about our rehearsal or concert. After a long delay, a grumbling caretaker turned up with a huge key and reluctantly let us in. When we finally got into the theatre, we discovered that the stage set had been left from the previous night's opera, *Aida*. We arranged our chairs and music stands and rehearsed while peeping around statues of elephants, palm trees and pyramids. These were eventually reluctantly cleared away just before our concert.

There were many similar 'mismanagements'. When yet another managerial disaster occurred, he was often heard to say, 'Oh no, it's another ACFU'(a colossal fuck up). He was beginning to get very stressed and Giles, his assistant, suggested that they should both get well away from the orchestra on the free day we all had in Vienna.

At the beginning of the day, they were to be found on a secluded hillside, overlooking a small lake, having a picnic. They were beginning to relax and enjoy the peaceful scene. It was not to last. The first thing they heard was shouts of laughter from the lake, and then a small rowing boat came into view. In the boat were Connor and the principal cellist. The boat was slowly sinking into the lake. The cellist had pulled a bung out of the bottom of the boat, just to see what would happen. The boat finally sank and as they waded towards the shore, the management team fled.

I spent seven years with the BBC. There were many great moments, and a few concerts that are indelibly fixed in my memory. After an overnight train journey, we arrived sleep-deprived in Vienna to play a morning concert. It could have been a lacklustre performance, but the Bartok *Concerto for Orchestra*, under Boulez's baton, took off and soared into the stratosphere.

There was also a fantastic Dvorak 9th Symphony under the baton of Rudolf Kempe at a Royal Albert Hall Promenade concert. This lovely symphony has been played many times and can sometimes become clichéd. It was applauded by an enraptured audience for a very long time. All musicians can replay their great concerts in their heads; sadly, sometimes, we can remember our not-so-good ones just as vividly.

BOULEZ AND ME

Many years later I was playing 2nd tuba with the LSO. I was only required in one piece: Stravinsky's *Rite of Spring*. The conductor was Pierre Boulez. The LSO were courting him fairly assiduously. His 80th birthday was coming up – good for ticket sales – and he was being looked after by the board of directors. He had given me a wave across the orchestra, but I hadn't had a chance to talk to him.

The flight home was delayed and I was sitting in the airport having some food and a glass of wine. Boulez was walking along with his group when he spotted me. He walked over to my table and asked if he could join me?

'Please do,' I said. He sat down and the members of the board stood behind him looking a little uncomfortable. Not knowing my history with him, I suspect they thought I might say something indiscreet.

Boulez said, 'Do you know it is twenty-three years since we played this piece together?' I noted that his precise memory certainly hadn't lost any of its edge. He had conducted the BBC only a few times since he had left them. As I often worked with them, he wanted to know all about the characters. He showed remarkably concise recall of all our BBC days and we had a lot of laughs. Our flight was called, but before he was ushered away, the last thing I said to him was, 'You must admit that the LSO's behaviour is much better these days than the BBC's was then.'

He looked at me and grinned. 'Who cares, they were good days.'

MAGIC POWERS

When I joined the BBC, one of the biggest characters in the orchestra was the 1st trombone. He was from Poland and told us often contradictory but always interesting stories of his life. Before the war he had been forcibly enrolled into the German army when he was just sixteen. They were visiting his village and his father had proudly told the army bandmaster that his son was a talented viola player. He was then promptly told that his son would now be joining their band as a trombone player. The stories were told over many late nights in hotel rooms while we were touring. As there wasn't anybody to verify them,

I suppose he may have felt free to elaborate. Perhaps he had been in dangerous situations during the war and had got into the habit of being economical with the truth. His favourite story was that after joining the German army band, he had escaped, joined the Polish army and been sent to Scotland on military exercises. Here he had met a girl from Caithness, and married her.

His great passion was for vodka. He reasoned that as it was a clear liquid (like water) it was fine. Not being the most logical of people, in his attempts to cut down on his cigarette consumption he cut them in half and smoked them to the last millimetre in a holder. A sure indication that he was feeling tired and emotional was that his normally well-combed fringe would fall down in front of his eyes. His powers of recovery, however, were remarkable.

When he began slurring his speech and muttering what sounded like Polish curses, we would try to figure out how to persuade the management that he was ill while trying to persuade him that he shouldn't play in the concert. The members of the orchestra who had seen this before were quite relaxed about the situation. Those of us who hadn't, imagined the concert was facing imminent disaster. Then he would produce his 'magic comb' and very carefully comb his hair. The dark mutterings would stop, and he would quietly get ready for the concert, which he would play very well indeed. To this day I don't know if this was a prepared act, or if his comb really was magic.

The good times rolled, but so did the bad. Some of the older members of the orchestra had become embittered, and this was particularly true of one very talented brass player who spread dissatisfaction to other players.

I had joined the London Sinfonietta and nearly all of the music they played was newly composed, or very modern. It was regarded by us all as an interesting challenge. A few of the unhappier BBC members seem to have two main grumbles, which became their mantras: if a piece had been written recently (in the last forty years), it probably wasn't worth playing; and most of the great conductors were now dead.

Eventually I found this a bit of a bore. I realised that I was having a better time doing sessions and working with other orchestras, so after seven years with the BBC I resigned.

CHAPTER 9

ESCAPE FROM THE RAT RACE?

For a period of my life, I seemed to be having the 'Midas touch' in reverse. Freelancers love to be busy but I forever seemed to be on the verge of breaking the cardinal rule, 'never be late'. Recording sessions cannot start until all of the players are present. If I drove to a gig there were serious traffic jams. If I attempted to travel by train, tube or bus all were suffering from major cancellations. The strain was getting me down.

Out of the blue I got a phone call from an old college mate. He was the manager of an orchestra north of London. Their tuba player was leaving and he had heard that I was getting a bit fed up; would I like to do a week with his orchestra to see if I enjoyed it? This seemed to me a great idea – far shorter travel, less work and a regular salary. A house that would be better and bigger than our present one for half the price.

We found a mutually good time and he booked me for a week's work with the orchestra. A friend of mine had been in this orchestra but had left after a year. I phoned him for some inside info. He told me that I would find the players, especially the brass section, set in their ways. They were very likely to give you their opinions, whether you wanted them or not; however, they were reluctant to actually act on their views. My friend said he had privately nicknamed the brass section 'The Hotbed of Apathy'. 'Good luck,' he said as he put the phone down.

Intrigued, I arrived at the first morning's rehearsal. They didn't seem particularly welcoming. At the break one of the brass section rushed to the subsidised canteen to get teas and coffees. When we sat down each of the players handed over their money to the person who had bought them – 20p for a coffee and 15p for a tea. At the next break I ran to 'get them in' for the section. I fancied a bit of chocolate so I bought two bars of Kit-Kat as well. They joined me and started to hand over their 15p and 20p. 'Please don't bother,' I said, 'I am here all week so I am sure it will work out.'

There was a silence, then Harold, clearly the group spokesman, said, 'That's not how we do it here, and besides,' he pointed accusingly at the two bars of Kit-Kat, 'What are those doing there?' I explained that I had got them to share. 'That's all very well,' he said, 'but who is going to pay for them?'

'Don't worry, I paid for them,' I said. Another silence!

This orchestra always had an hour and a half for lunch; all of the other orchestras I worked for only ever had an hour. On day three, I asked someone, why the extra half-hour? I was curious if this was for a specific reason. I was accused of trying to upset the system and that they weren't happy with my 'fancy London ideas'.

After the final rehearsal I passed Harold sitting in his car, which was parked at a meter. I waved and he reluctantly wound down his window. 'You do know the rehearsal has finished, Harold?' I asked, tongue in cheek.

'I am fully aware of that fact, young man, but I have paid for three hours' parking and I am not going to leave this meter until my time is up.'

After the concert I packed my car and set off in record time. As I drove back towards London, my smile became broader. I have never seen any of them again.

SIDNEY SAX

Lots of music for films is recorded in Britain – in fact, the majority of music for American films is also done in London. British players have a reputation for being quick and good, and we are also a lot cheaper than our US counterparts. By far the most successful fixer of these films and most of the commercial sessions, when I moved to London, was a man called Sidney Sax. He had risen, or rather elbowed, his way to the top of this particularly lucrative field, in a ruthless and shrewd way.

While a lot of fixers were, to put it mildly, unreliable – we regularly came across post-dated cheques, cheques that bounced, seriously late payments, or sometimes no payments at all - Sid always paid cash at the end of all his sessions. He was a successful violinist himself, and it was rumoured that he had initially borrowed the money to pay for the sessions, knowing that musicians would do his work for prompt cash payments.

At the end of each day's work, we would line up after the gig and give Sid our invoices. He would scrutinise them very carefully, then even more carefully count out the money. We would then mentally doff our caps, and thank him effusively, but not too effusively, as he might decide that we were trying to curry favour with him. Shirley, his wife, would double-check the payments. We used to joke that any offence caused to Sid would elicit the sotto voce response, 'Cross him off the list, Shirley'.

Film sessions were by far the best-paid work around. When the buy-out (one payment for all the uses of the music, i.e. TV, CDs, radio and everything else) was introduced, film-session payments were roughly three times the amount we received for doing concerts or classical recordings. Everybody wanted to do film sessions and a lot of the principal wind, strings and brass players from the major London orchestras had left to work for Sid.

He was a tough businessman and he was aware of the situation he had created. His main players had to do what he wanted, whenever he wanted it. If one of his players had booked a family holiday, and Sid offered him some last-minute work, then the player had to cancel the holiday. Those who didn't, often found that they weren't phoned again. He demanded total loyalty from his regular players, which wasn't reciprocated by his loyalty to any of them.

Sid used to lead all of his own sessions (this became his downfall later). Sitting behind him in the first violins, Sid would often have all the leaders of the London orchestras.

One of the trumpeters saw that Sid had left his keys in the ignition after showing off his new car to some of the players. He took the keys and gave them back to Sid in front of the orchestra, fully expecting to be thanked. Sid took them and didn't say a word. Not a good move, said a shrewd friend of mine, shaking his head. That player wasn't booked by Sid for four years.

At the end of a session one day, we all queued up to receive our money. Sid had been called away and Shirley was paying us. There had been fifteen minutes' overtime on the session, and Shirley had told us that the overtime fee was £12.16. A player in front of me had just received his fee, when Sid arrived back. He looked over his wife's shoulder, then started. 'What's this, Shirley?' he demanded.

'Oh, that's the fifteen minutes' overtime, Sid,' she explained.

'That's not right,' he said. 'Fifteen minutes' overtime should be £12.09p, not £12.16p.'

'Oh Sid,' said Shirley, looking like she was going to faint from the shock, 'I am very sorry.'

I was just about to be paid, but time seemed to stand still. Feeling that I should say something, I said, 'Never mind Sid, It's only money.'

Sid and Shirley stared at me. They both looked like they wanted to kill me.

You would expect, then, that anyone who took advantage of Sid and his world of money, would get the 'never again'. A percussionist friend of mine, Eric, did a lot of work for Sid. At the end of a session, as he was putting his instruments away, he got paid twice - once by Shirley, and again later by Sid. He didn't say anything about it.

Two weeks later, at the end of another session, Sid approached him. 'Eric, you're a bit of a sly one, aren't you?'

Eric looked at him, smiled and said, 'Why is that, Sid?'

'Well, two weeks ago I paid you for a session, and so did Shirley.'

Eric said, 'Is that right, Sid?'

There was a pause, then Sid said, 'So what are we going to do about that then?' There was silence, then Sid said, 'I tell you what to do, put down double the fee for today, then you can give me half.' At no point did Sid expect Eric to pay back the money he owed him. Perhaps he had recognised a kindred spirit.

Players of large instruments – harps, double basses, percussion, tubas and cellos – get paid porterage for transporting their instruments. It goes towards the extra cost of taxis and parking, etc., and is paid at the end of the sessions. Porterage is considered essential, as getting harps, timpani, percussion and double basses onto public transport would be impossible. The fixer will have charged the contracting company for the porterage in advance.

At the end of one five-day work period, we all queued up for our money. Sid played his new principal double bass player his fee, plus five days' porterage. He hadn't worked for Sid before, and was obviously trying to impress him (wrong). He said he only wanted one day's porterage as he had left his bass here for five days. The rest of us looked at him with horror, as we had also left our instruments in the studios for five days but were claiming porterage for five days. Sid stared at him in disbelief, and total incomprehension. The main purpose in Sid's life was making money, and here was a man asking for less of the stuff. He was speechless for several seconds, then he paid the player a single day's porterage and never booked him again.

I continued to work for Sid, but often felt uneasy about it. It wasn't because of my feelings about his lack of integrity but because of his expectation that you would drop everything, including other bookings, to do his work. As he was sometimes paying more money than the orchestras, he wouldn't accept any reason for you not to do his work. 'Get out of that, I pay better than they do,' was his reasoning. If you were committed to doing all of his work, you were stuck without a choice.

A very fine flute player, who had been principal flute of a London orchestra, had left to work exclusively for Sid. Later he discovered he had got cancer and had to have time off for treatment. When he was given the all clear, he phoned Sid to give him the good news. Sid said to him, 'I am not prepared to take the risk of you getting ill again, so I have replaced you with another flute player.'

Eventually I told Sid that I wasn't prepared to cancel other gigs just to do his. I realised that this probably would be the end of my connection with him. After that only a few dates came to me when he was stuck for a player. I felt a lot better knowing I could choose my own gigs, even though I was financially the loser.

CHAPTER 10

THE ROYAL OPERA HOUSE

Sir Antonio Pappano was due to conduct a run of a new opera – *The Minotaur*, written by Harrison Birtwistle. The office of the Opera House had booked me to do the run. Three days before the main rehearsals were due to start, they phoned me and asked if I could do a brass sectional rehearsal

With Sir Antonio Pappano and George Wall

I turned up at the Opera House and went to the pit, which was empty. I tried the main rehearsal room, also empty. I phoned the office, who told me that the brass sectional rehearsal was going to be held in Pappano's room. I had never been there but reflected that he must have a huge room if he could get a large brass section in there. I found the room, and there was Pappano and one brass player – George Wall, the Opera House's tuba player. We looked at the tuba parts and apart from the opening of the opera we didn't seem to have a lot to play. He whispered to me that it probably wouldn't take long, and started planning our lunch. It turned out that the 'brass sectional' was just for the two tubas. Three hours later we finished. Pappano was keen for more and asked us to do another rehearsal the next day, at 8 a.m., but George asked to push it back until later that morning when the two of us – who were both in our sixties – could travel in for free. I don't suppose Sir Antonio Pappano, a rich and famous international conductor, spent a lot of time worrying about free public transport.

TWO GRIM OPERAS BY ALBAN BERG

I had been booked to do a run of on-stage bands with the Royal Opera House at Covent Garden Stage bands usually have wind and brass or just strings. This particular band had an unusual orchestration: four violins, one accordion, one clarinet, a guitar and a tuba. We were supposed to be a Heuriger (a German tavern band) and we were given very shabby clothes to wear; we were supposed to be a group who had seen much better days, but were now down at heel. We had to go onto the stage for about five minutes to play the tavern scene. The terrifying bit was that we had to play our music from memory. This opera, *Wozzeck*, was written by the Austrian composer Alban Berg in the 1920s. One critic described it as an opera that contained 'abrupt, stark and brutal language, prostitution, violence and murder'. Wozzeck's wife is raped by a soldier, then she takes up with him.

Wozzeck threatens to beat her and she says to him, 'Better a knife in my belly than your hands on me.' Wozzeck becomes obsessed with the idea of using a knife. Later in a tavern, he finds her dancing with her soldier. He takes her to a lake and stabs her. He goes back to the tavern, where the other customers see that his hands and arms are covered in blood and they drive him away. He goes back to the lake to wash off the blood, falls into the lake and drowns.

The Opera House was looking for a young boy to play the part of Wozzeck's son. Liz, a musician friend of mine, whose son sang well, took him to the audition and he was offered the part. She was asked if she would like to look after him for the duration of the run, or have special chaperones from the company to look after him. She still didn't know anything at all about the plot of the opera. As she had got a lot of work in, she thought that this would be fine and asked them to chaperone him. Liz didn't attend any of the rehearsals, so still didn't know the story, but her son always came back from rehearsals very happy, saying he was having a good time.

She was invited to the first night's performance, and as she watched the grim story unfold, she became more and more horrified. The opera ends with the boy sitting alone on the stage, singing a solo. Behind him, lying in a tank of water, is his drowned father. She began to question herself, and had a huge attack of guilt. What sort of a mother was she? Surely, she had traumatised her ten-year-old son for life? Then she thought, but after all the rehearsals he had said it was a lot of fun! At the end of the show, in great trepidation, she made her way to his dressing room. She found him with the soloists, laughing, eating sweets and telling them silly jokes, which they all seemed to be enjoying enormously.

A similar dark opera, *Lulu*, also written by Alban Berg was being performed at the London Coliseum by the English National Opera company. Like *Wozzeck* it is a story that contains a lot of angst. A high-born lady, the mistress of a rich man, descends into the gutter and becomes a street prostitute.

One night, a coach-load of pensioners arrived. Within ten minutes of the opera starting, they stormed the box office, demanding their money back. They were members of the Lulu fan club – the Scottish pop singer – and had come expecting an evening of her greatest hits. It really was a case of 'Everybody shout now' at the box office. Luckily they all got their money back.

LSO AND STOKOWSKI – SID SAX AGAIN

In 1973, I was doing some work with the LSO, recording Mahler's 2nd Symphony. The conductor was Leopold Stokowski, who had risen to great fame many years before in Hollywood. He was the 'Maestro' in Disney's *Fantasia*. It was Disney's full-length musical animation film. Stokowski had arranged and orchestrated the music, and was not only seen conducting the orchestra, but also having a conversation with Mickey Mouse.

According to Stokowski's biography, he had been born in Marylebone in 1882 and was an 'English conductor of Polish descent'. He clearly was a seriously talented musician, and at the age of thirteen had gone to study at the Royal College of Music, then to Queen's College Oxford. This didn't explain his strange foreign accent. He later went on to win great acclaim in America.

The LSO would definitely have had more sympathy for him if he had been a nicer man, but he had started to work with them on an unfortunate footing. One of the older players with the orchestra told me about the first time he had come to conduct them and why the band were wary of him.

On his first visit to the orchestra, halfway through the rehearsal, he stopped, and said to them, 'You sirs, you have *Kinder*?' The orchestra were mystified until it was explained that Stokowski wanted to know if they had children. He asked the principal viola if he had *Kinder*, and the viola player admitted he did indeed, then the maestro asked the orchestra to put up their hands if they had children. 'You bring your *Kinder* to the rehearsal tomorrow and they can watch us making great music together.' The next day some of the players brought their children to the rehearsal and sat them in the hall. The maestro arrived and insisted that all of the '*Kinder*' must sit next to their parents in the orchestra. All of these players were then told many times that they were not 'playing their best' and were humiliated in front of their children.

This had happened many years before. This time, when we tried to record Mahler's 2nd Symphony, Stokowski was ninety and had had a stroke. While he still seemed mentally OK, his speech was a bit hard to understand and his conducting rather haphazard.

It wasn't a good experience; it seemed grossly unfair to put him through this task and most of the musicians ended up feeling sorry for him. In spite of the excellent playing of the LSO, the misleading conducting made it impossible for them to finish the recording. The players felt that the whole thing was demeaning for all concerned and the sessions were finally abandoned.

Enter Sidney Sax, who didn't suffer from such scruples, particularly not if there was money involved. So, two years later, I found myself again playing for Stokowski – now aged ninety-two - with the Sidney Sax Orchestra.

He had become even frailer and his temper hadn't improved. He arrived accompanied by an oleaginous, sycophantic carer/assistant, who told us, in his high, shrill American accent, that we'd have to stand 'in silence' while Stokowski made his way to the rostrum, and then sit.

The maestro appeared and we were fixed by the steely eye of the leader, Sid Sax, as Stokowski walked very unsteadily to the rostrum. This seemed to take an extraordinarily long time. The temptation to hum the 'Dead March' from *Saul* was strong, but no one dared.

It took an even longer time until he was settled by his fussing assistant, who sat on a stool in front of the rostrum, which held the scores. Stokowski muttered something incomprehensible, and we were told in shrill tones by his assistant that we would first record the March from Berlioz's *Damnation of Faust*. We were given a strange sideways hand gesture which was followed by silence from the players and shouts of anger from the maestro. These were followed by aggrieved instructions from the lackey. 'The maestro insists that you all start on his beat.' What beat? Another sideways gesture followed, and with a huge downbow from Sid, we started to play.

We faltered on, playing a few bars, stopping, listing to angry mumbling from the maestro and asinine statements from his assistant. Unfortunately, Stokowski's co-ordination had got so bad that he couldn't manage to turn over the pages of the score in front of him. His assistant clearly wasn't allowed to do this, so each page would be held up so that the maestro could make a sort of sideways swipe, to finish turning it over. This seemed to work, more or less, but everyone was getting fed up with the assistant and his apparent bewilderment that we couldn't follow the conducting.

While we were playing, the maestro was doing hand gestures totally unrelated to the music, and the lackey was holding up each page of the score. We were making progress until Stokowski could no longer turn one of the pages, at which point the lackey took it upon himself to step in and turn the page himself.

With a shout of anger, the maestro turned and clouted his assistant across the head. This made a loud slapping sound, followed by silence. 'Ah,' I thought, 'the sweet sound of one hand clapping.'

Sid always insisted on leading all of his own sessions and this was ultimately his downfall. Chuck (Charles) Gerhard always used Sid and his orchestra for all the films that he brought to Britain. One particular film called for some virtuoso violin solos and the sponsors had not been happy with Sid's playing. Chuck had told Sid that he was always happy to use Sid's orchestra, if he could book one of the virtuoso violin players to play the solos if necessary. Sid retorted that if Chuck ever wanted his orchestra, it would always have to be led by him. This was probably the beginning of the end of all of Sid's work.

THE DEMON DRINK

I was on my second three-week tour of America. It had been enjoyable, but it had started to seem very long. I was missing my young family and was desperate to see them. The last concert of the trip was in Toronto and I had arranged to stay there for three days to spend time with my parents, my sister and the rest of the family, who had by now lived there for many years.

The previous night we had been playing in New York and some of our American brass-playing friends had invited us to a party. We didn't have to leave until the next day at noon so a party seemed like a great idea.

One of our richer musician friends had a penthouse. We were taken there and given food and cocktails in hugely generous, liver-crippling amounts. I finally got to bed at 3 a.m. I set two alarms, arranged back-up calls all round, and passed out.

I woke up at 8 a.m. feeling great, probably because I was still drunk. We checked out of the hotel, got a bus to the airport, hung around, then got the plane to Toronto, and finally a bus from the airport to the venue, which was in Ontario Place. By then, I was feeling dreadful, and I was reminding myself why I usually didn't drink spirits. The alcohol was wearing off, and the hangovers were kicking in. I avoided a hair of the dog, and hoped I'd make it through the concert.

My whole family had turned up – parents, sister, brother-in-law, nieces, nephews, friends – to see us play. Our concert was in The Forum, a large covered bandstand in Ontario Place, just by the CN Tower, on the banks of Lake Ontario. The orchestra sat in the middle of the auditorium, with the audience surrounding us, and we got ready to play some film and TV themes. The concert was scheduled to last for an hour without any interval.

I sat down feeling shocking. I waved back to my madly waving family, causing me to have a sensation as if my brain had dislodged itself and was moving around in the inside of my head. My family were seated directly in front of me. I opened my music and thought, just sixty minutes and then I can have a drink.

The concert started and I focused on my music. After about fifteen minutes I had a tacet number (I wasn't needed). I looked in front of me to see how my family was but they weren't there. A wave of panic washed over me and I thought, this is it, I am never drinking again. I looked left, then right, and there they were. I tried to persuade myself that they really hadn't been sitting in front of me at the start of the concert, they had always been sitting on my right all the time. The next time I looked for them on my right, they weren't there. Panic. I looked in front, to my left, then right, then behind me. There they were, waving and smiling.

By the time the concert finished they were sitting in front of me again. I expect most of you by now will have guessed what was happening, but I was in no state to figure it out. I vowed that this was going to be the first temperance day for the rest of my life, and that the strongest thing I would ever drink in future would be tea.

I put my tuba away and feeling seriously shaky, I went to find my family. They had loved the concert, particularly the way the stage revolved. With relief I toasted that revelation with a drink…not of tea.

THE LONDON SINFONIETTA

Another of my regular gigs was with the London Sinfonietta. They had been formed in 1974 and I had played with them from the start. They specialised in new music, much of which was composed especially for them.

The composer Mauricio Kagel often came to conduct the London Sinfonietta, and always brought one of his compositions with him. His pieces were often unusual and interesting, and among my favourites was *1814*.

He had commissioned a faithful re-creation of the room in which Beethoven had written many of his compositions. Each of the items in the room was papered with pages from Beethoven's piano sonatas. About 25 of these pages had been photographed and reproduced in a booklet, which each player was given. If the notes on the paper were clear then we played them. When they were blurred, we'd play them in an out-of-focus way. Kagel would hold up a page number for a few of us and we'd play it. The piece was appealing and it was different each time we played it. We got the giggles in the initial rehearsals, but Kagel didn't seem to mind.

However, he did get cross with us at our next concert. We were performing one of his pieces in the hall at the University of Brussels, where he was the resident composer. This piece was written for nine different instruments and was composed in a conventional way but with some complexities that called for great concentration.

I don't know to this day if we had been set up by two of his students. We were sitting at one end of the hall, on the same level as the audience, who were quite close to us. Apparently, they were mostly Kagel's composition students. As we were about to play, a young couple walked in, and sat in the front row. As we played, they started kissing. Things began to heat up: he put his hand up her blouse, she put her hand down his trousers. We were so distracted that we barely managed to keep going. We just about got to the end of the piece.

Kagel was not amused.

I was beginning a rehearsal at the QEH (Queen Elizabeth Hall), with the London Sinfonietta. We were playing a new composition written for ten different instruments. We had been arranged on the stage in a semi-circle, and dancers would weave around us while we played. In order to get a good sound balance each of us had separate microphones. The rehearsal began, each of us playing in turn. We played bits from our parts, which were mostly strange atonal noises with effects. There was a very young-looking cellist that I had never seen before. As he was sitting next to me, I introduced myself and he told me his name was Paul. When it was his turn to play, he played the strange effects from his part, and then the producer stopped him. He explained that as the cello had the most to play, he needed to hear him play a continuous tune for a while so that he could get a good balance. Paul started to play the lovely Andante, the third movement from Elgar's Cello Concerto. He began to play very quietly, almost tentatively. As he played, he seemed to grow in confidence. The background noises of the stage hands, cleaners and dancers grew quiet, and we listened with rapt attention to this wonderful sound; a lot of us were very near to tears. Eventually he was asked to stop.

I asked him where he played regularly, and he giggled. 'Nowhere really. I just started studying music at Cambridge last year. I wanted to know how my standard would compare with professional players, so I did an audition for the back-desk cello position with the BBC Symphony Orchestra.' I asked him how he had got on and he giggled again. 'Well, they told me that they didn't want to offer the back-desk position, but asked me if I would accept the principal cello position.' Paul Watkins became their principal cellist and worked there for seven years.

CHAPTER 11

TWO GIGS. BOTH EMBARRASSING.

Backing music for TV was mostly played by real musicians as opposed to synthesised as it is today. It paid well, especially if the band was also being filmed. One TV fixer, Frank, was a clarinet player, and like many jazz/light music players also played the flute and all of the saxophone family, from the soprano to the bass sax.

Frank offered me two days' playing, which would be filmed. I couldn't do the first day, so he said he would have to try someone else as it was tied work, and he needed to find someone who could do both days. He later phoned to book me for the second of the two days, as he hadn't found anyone for both. When I turned up to do the session, he told me I'd just be miming as they had done all the recording the day before and that he'd actually played the tuba part on bass sax.

I opened the music and saw there was a solo for tuba. We started filming and as the camera came closer to me, I had to pretend to be playing, while being accompanied by some awful bass sax playing. Short of fainting, I knew I couldn't do anything to escape from this so I carried on. I didn't see the finished programme. I have erased the name of it from my mind and I hope nobody I know has seen it.

I do tell my next experience with embarrassment. There was to be a huge extravaganza concert at Drury Lane Theatre. It was presented by Petula Clark and was to feature a Russian Circus troupe (the Panovs), world-famous artistes, singers, comedians and dancers. It was going to be simultaneously filmed and broadcast throughout Europe, with the recordings sold to many more countries, so there was serious money attached to it.

I was only needed for one piece and had to play two notes twice, in a shortened piece of ballet music written by Jack Lanchbery, taken from his ballet, *La Fille Mal Gardée* – the famous 'Clog Dance'.

The pit was full of doubling instruments, saxes, clarinets, flutes, so there was no room for me. It was decided that a chair and a music stand would be placed at the side of the pit just before my piece began. I was to walk in at the end of the previous piece, sit, play my two notes twice, then leave. I spent the whole day walking in and out of the theatre, and the pub. Each time I got back to the rehearsal I heard 'tuba not needed yet, go away,' so I'd go back to the pub. Eventually they ran out of time, so I never got to do a rehearsal.

Before the show I changed and waited to hear the piece that was to be my cue to walk on, the number before the one I was due to play, but suddenly I heard the 'Clog Dance' begin. They had changed the order of the programme. I looked into the theatre and saw that my stand and chair had been placed in position by the side of the pit. I started to walk along the edge of the stalls, towards my chair, carrying my tuba. As I approached the pit, I heard the piece end. I watched as my music stand and chair were carried away. I turned and walked slowly back to the dressing room. No one noticed. I did get paid.

THREE FUN TV GIGS

1. HAPPY CHRISTMAS MR BEAN

I was asked to be in a Salvation Army (SA) band for the filming of *Happy Christmas Mr Bean*. There were four players –

cornet, tenor horn, euphonium and tuba. We played two traditional carols and one jazzed-up one. We had two rehearsals with Rowan Atkinson, who was conducting it, and he worked assiduously, discussing the music and trying different comedic gestures.

The final filming of the show was going to be in the Kingston apple market in the late evening. The whole day was going to be spent doing location shots of the SA band in uniform, standing together and pretending to play. I was asked if I would like to do this but I didn't fancy it; the fee wasn't good and I didn't want to stand in the cold all day.

They wanted to borrow my tuba for someone else to hold during the day's location shots. I had visions of it lying on the ground and a large camera trolley running over it, so I declined. Then they said they would hire a tuba from a local music shop, and get an extra to wear my SA uniform.

Having had a good warm day at home, I turned up for the evening's filming. I went into our dressing room and saw a man struggling to get out of my SA uniform, which was too small for him. He then peeled off the false beard that he been wearing all day and I realised that he was my double.

He had the biggest, heaviest tuba I have ever seen, and he'd had to hold up this cold, lumpen object all day long. 'Ah, you must be me,' I said. In response, he shot me a filthy look.

We did some filming and playing with our band and after some meticulous re-takes with Rowan Atkinson, we were told to have a short break but to stay in costume.

Fancying a drink, I went into the local pub and ordered a Guinness. The elderly barmaid came very close to me, looked around and said very quietly, 'You do know that Guinness is alcoholic, don't you, dear.' I laughed and told her that I wasn't really in the Salvation Army. She served me, but it was clear she doubted my word.

Happy Christmas Mr Bean seems to be shown most Christmases in some part of the world or on a plane. My sister often phones me from Canada to tell me she has seen it again. I'd have made some money if it had been a job with repeat fees, but sadly it wasn't!

2. MR OOM-PAH-PAH

I got a call to play the sousaphone as 'Mr Oom-pah-pah' for the children's TV show *Rainbow*. My children loved the show, so I was familiar with the characters. There was Mr Geoffrey, in his chef's outfit, reading stories in his kitchen; Bungle and Zippy; and Rod, Jane and Freddy, the singing trio. Mr Geoffrey read the story of Mr Oom-pah-pah and I played the sousaphone. I was given a shaker for the play-out at the end of the programme, and I danced around the kitchen, shaking my shaker and felt a right prat. My children loved it, my wife less so, and when I actually watched it, I realised that perhaps it wouldn't be an actor's life for me.

3. HERCULE POIROT

They were making an episode of *Hercule Poirot* called 'The Italian Stallion', and they needed a band of four players to lead a wedding procession through Kensington Roof Gardens. The musicians in the band played accordion, clarinet, trumpet and tuba. We had to march, followed by the bride and groom and guests. If you've ever seen any Poirot you'll know that it is always perfectly presented and costumed. From the outset the producer was very unhappy with the way John Barclay, the trumpet player, and I looked. All the cast looked Italian – perfectly dressed, dark-haired, olive-skinned. All of the cast except for John and me, that is. Each time the producer saw us, he was upset. We were taken for a haircut and were paid to have it. Then they dyed our hair and sent us back to make-up. Nothing worked, and when I finally saw it, I could see why the producer was so unhappy: after all his efforts, we still looked like a couple of ruddy-faced Manchester butchers.

THREE NOT SO ENJOYABLE GIGS

1. BOOED OFF THE STAGE IN PARIS

I was due to do two concerts at the Champs-Elysées theatre in Paris with the LSO, under Claudio Abbado. The heavy brass (trombones and tuba) were not needed until after the interval. The first half of the concert had been well received and we went onto the platform to play Tchaikovsky's 4th Symphony with a good sense of anticipation. We started to play the opening fanfare of the symphony with lots of energy but the audience started booing. As we played, the booing got louder, with cries of 'Malheur!' None of us knew what this really meant; I discovered later it meant 'unfortunate'! We began to play progressively louder, but after we had played the first thirty bars, Abbado angrily flung down his baton and stalked off the stage, indicating to the orchestra that we should follow him.

The French theatre manager came on to the stage and announced to the audience that the incorrect dates had been printed on the programmes and that we couldn't play Mahler's 5th as advertised as we didn't have the full complement of musicians. They were given the choice of a refund or staying to listen to the Tchaikovsky. Most people stayed.

We were in good company as Stravinsky's first performance of *The Rite of Spring* had been booed by the audience in the same theatre, in 1913. I actually admired the way the French audience voiced its discontent. An English audience might have stayed to listen to the performance and then quietly grumbled.

2. GREAT BIG STAR

I was looking forward to doing a week's film sessions in Barnes Bridge. Though it was a very scruffy studio, where everything was falling apart – doors, windows, microphones held together by miles of gaffer tape – Keith, the balancer, always seem to produce incredible good quality recordings. The music was written and conducted by Michel Le Grand.

The Great Big Star was handed out of a limousine and looked a bit shocked when she saw the outside of the studio. When she went in, she was appalled and everything seemed to go downhill from there. Every song was in the wrong key, she didn't like the sound of the orchestra and on day two she told the players that they were not allowed in the recording booth to listen to the takes we had made. The rest of the week passed, for her, very unhappily. The takes we had heard were excellent but she took them away and re-recorded them somewhere else. Great artist – what a shame.

3. MARIA CALLAS

We were due to do some recording with Maria Callas. Martin, a flute player friend of mine, had been completely in love with her voice. He had studied flute as a student with Jean-Pierre Rampal in Paris while Callas was living there and had often gone without food so he could go to one of her recitals.

I expected him to be delighted that we would now be performing with her, but he said he felt trepidation that her voice wouldn't be the wonderful instrument it had been and that he would be left feeling sad and disappointed. He was right.

The recording was at St Giles' Church. From the outset it was tragic. Callas was in a very nervous state. Her high notes were really insecure and realising she was singing badly, she became progressively worse. Martin was nearly in tears, remembering the Callas he had heard as a student. In her heyday, Callas had received a forty-minute standing ovation at the end of one of her Covent Garden performances from an enraptured audience.

Eventually the recordings we had been attempting to make were abandoned. Two years later Callas was discovered dead in her Paris flat. A very sad end to an immensely special talent.

CHAPTER 12

THE EMBASSY

Modern composers often write complicated and difficult parts for the tuba. As the players get progressively better, composers enjoy using their virtuosity. However, a lot of more traditional composers often just use the tuba in their pieces to reinforce the bass section. I had been asked to play probably one of the shortest tuba parts ever written with the Philharmonia Orchestra at the Royal Festival Hall: Dvorak's Symphony No. 9, *From the New World*. The tuba part has just fourteen notes, doubled with the bass trombone. Seven notes are played at the beginning of the second movement and seven at the end – before and after the lovely cor anglais solo.

Vladimir Ashkenazy, the wonderful pianist, had just started to conduct and this was to be one of his first dates on the rostrum. The orchestra were giving a benefit concert to raise funds for a concert hall in Reykjavik. Like most benefit concerts, it was to be attended by VIPs, including Prince Charles, Princess Diana and the president of Iceland.

I was only involved in the second half of the concert, with my fourteen notes. I arrived before the interval and changed into my waistcoat, white tie and tails. At the interval, two friends from Iceland, who'd been invited to the concert, came to say hello and asked if I could take them home, as they lived close to me. I said I was happy to give them a lift, but that I wanted to make a quick getaway after the concert, and wouldn't be getting changed. We agreed to meet at the backstage lift as soon after the concert finished as they could manage. I played my notes and just after the end of the concert my friends arrived at the lift. As we were about to get into it, we were stopped by security and made to wait while the VIPs were shepherded past us: the Prince and Princess of Wales, then Iceland's president, with the splendid name Vigdís Finnbogadóttir. She spotted my friends and started a conversation with them in Icelandic, seemingly inviting them to a party. She turned to me and said 'But of course you must come too.'

I explained that my car was parked on the street. After a chat with security, we were taken to it. We got into my small green Ford and joined the procession of black official cars, flanked by a police motorbike escort. It turned out we were going to a reception party at the Icelandic Embassy. I assumed that some of the orchestra would also be there but when we arrived, I discovered that the only other musician there was Ashkenazy, dressed casually in a green roll-neck sweater. I was still wearing my concert gear so everyone gathered round me, clearly believing that I was the only member of the orchestra there and so, presumably, the leader. After a short time, the prime minister called for silence and then thanked me for my 'wonderful expressive playing'. I just managed to stop myself asking her which of my fourteen notes she had enjoyed the most.

CHRISTMAS CAROLS IN JUNE

Musicians are very lucky – we generally really like what we do or we wouldn't do it. Sometimes we have reservations about the pieces we play but like any professional performers we just have to 'get on with it'. The next gig could be wonderful.

I have a great fondness for Christmas carols, for both the music and the words. 'Hark The Herald Angels Sing' … *Light and life to all he brings, risen with healing in his wings.* To me, these words remind me of this magic time of year; of childhood

Christmases; of hope; of getting out of the cold into a warm home; of the light shining through church windows.

I often worked for Nat Peck, an American fixer who had settled in London. He had been a trombonist with the Glenn Miller Band. Every year we would do two weeks of recording sessions for Nat, for an American friend of his, Brad Junior II. Brad would turn up with a large pile of Christmas carols and songs. He had arranged for these to be played in the lifts of Midwest Bible belt hotels. The first time I was booked, I was looking forward to hearing these. The only drawback was that every year he turned up, not at Christmastime but in June.

Brad was a large pleasant plump-ish man. He had a scrubbed pink florid face and blond hair and he always wore the same clothes: a sky-blue, one-piece garment that perfectly matched the colour of his eyes. In England at the time this was only worn by babies and was called a babygro (now apparently they're called 'onesies'). My youngest child, who was three, had just grown out of his.

Every June for two weeks Brad would turn up and bring the hot weather with him. We sweated our way through his arrangements of 'In The Bleak Mid-winter', 'See Amid The Winter's Snow', 'Chestnuts Roasting On An Open Fire' and other warming Christmas numbers, with Brad growing progressively pinker as he waved his arms around in the stuffy hot studio.

Somehow Brad's arrangements have taken the edge off the Christmas celebrations. I do have the odd nightmare at Christmastime. I imagine an enormous pink-faced man clad in a blue babygro suit, leaping around accompanied by strangely atonal Christmas music.

STAR WARS AND A SPECIAL TRUMPET PLAYER

Although I wasn't one of the people who shaped the history of film music, I am proud to say I was sometimes there when it happened. I was looking at an empty diary again (the freelancer's curse), when one Sunday evening the phone rang. It was the fixer for the LSO asking if I was free the following day. 'We are doing the music for a film called *Star Wars*,' he said. 'You'll just be needed for the morning. It's some sort of film about space, lots of battles and a man dressed in a dog suit. The conductor wants to try using an extra tuba.'

I asked who the conductor was, and was told John Williams.

'The guitarist?'

'No, not that John Williams. This one's American, and he also wrote the music.'

The sessions were at Denham and I was delighted to go back there. The recording studios were on the old film lot. They had stopped making films there some time before, but the sets were still intact. When I had previously worked there, I had spent my breaks wandering into these huge barns that contained the main street of a town from the Wild West, complete with saloon bars, banks, sheriff's office and jail, or Manhattan with the Chrysler building, the Empire State building and a giant model of King Kong.

I turned up the next day, looking forward to seeing a man in a dog suit and having a lunchtime wander. The film really did have a man in a dog suit, but it also had beautifully crafted music composed and conducted by John Williams, who was courteous but very particular and firm about the way he wanted us to play his music.

The LSO had just got a new 1st trumpet player – Maurice Murphy. I had known Maurice when I was at college, when he played in the BBC Northern Orchestra in Manchester. Before that, he had been the principal cornet player of the Black Dyke Mills Band – probably the most famous of all of the bands. He had been my boyhood hero when I first started playing in my local band.

While there were many fine cornet players in brass bands, few could play in orchestras because they could only play with vibrato and couldn't transpose parts at sight. Brass-band tradition calls for the players to nearly always play with vibrato and the parts are always transposed and written out for ease of reading. In the orchestra, trumpet players need to be able to sight-read in different keys and play with or without vibrato depending on the period or type of music they are playing.

Maurice had learned to play without vibrato and to transpose trumpet parts. He auditioned for the BBC Northern Orchestra in Manchester and had been accepted immediately. He had been very happy in the north, and despite many offers from London orchestras, it looked as though he was there to stay. Eventually the LSO had persuaded him to join them and his first booking was playing *Star Wars*.

As the sessions progressed John Williams would make meticulous changes to his music, but whenever the 1st trumpet played, he would ask, 'Say, first trumpet, can you put that bit up the octave?' 'Say, first trumpet, can you continue the flute melody there?' The reply would always be 'Yes, OK.'

At the end of every day John Williams would take away the 1st trumpet parts and add a lot more music to them. The more Maurice played the more John Williams liked it and the whole score changed. It was the beginning of heroic film music, which made the action on the screen much more exciting. It was followed by the second and third *Star Wars* films, then *Indiana Jones* – the list is long and it was mainly because of two men, one wonderful trumpet player and one great composer who was inspired to write increasingly adventurous music.

Later, I did some sessions for another film – *The Shape of Water*. Maurice Desplat was the composer and Maurice Murphy was playing trumpet. It was a small orchestra and getting smaller. On the final session, Maurice Desplat sent each player away when there wasn't any more music for us to play. We finished playing one last number, and he said, 'Thank you, I no longer need the first trumpet or the tuba.'

Maurice Murphy was giving me a lift home. As we walked towards his car, we saw the composer running towards us shouting for Maurice. Maurice thought he was being called back to play, but in fact Desplat had caught up with him for quite another matter. 'You are the reason I write film music,' he told him. From the man who had gone on on to write the music for *Harry Potter and the Deathly Hallows*, *The Imitation Game* and *Fantastic Mr Fox*, this was a great compliment to a great musician.

SCARY STUFF

I did some film music for a well-known film composer, Bernard Herrmann. I suppose his most famous film score had been for *Psycho*. Hitchcock had said that Herrmann's music made his all of his films at least 35% better.

We were recording the music for a film called *It's Alive*. The main star was Mia Farrow, who had been impregnated by the devil, and the 'It' of the title was their offspring.

Herrmann always used the same method of working. Before the orchestra even played the music, the musicians would be shown the relevant part of the film without any soundtrack. One of the takes showed the camera slowly panning in on an old-fashioned pram with a hood. As the camera got closer, a reptilian claw crept out from beneath the baby blankets. The first time we watched it, it seemed quite humorous and the orchestra laughed, much to the annoyance of Herrmann, though to be honest, he seemed annoyed a lot of the time. We rehearsed the music then recorded it. Then we were shown the film with the music. Within seconds, funny had become terrifying.

BUSKING

It was a cold, wet day and I was on my way to do a rehearsal with the Royal Opera House Orchestra in Covent Garden. I was standing on the platform of my local station with my tuba on my back and I was getting soaked. I noticed a man looking in my direction several times, then he walked over to me.

'That's a tuba, isn't it? I used to play the tuba, played it for a long time. I loved it.'

He seemed a pleasant man and I asked him if he still played. He said he'd stopped when he'd had a family as he couldn't make enough money to support them. He had retrained as a plumber and now had two businesses. He asked me where I was off to. It seemed pretentious to say 'I am going to play with Royal Opera House Orchestra', so I just said Covent Garden. His face fell. 'You shouldn't be out busking in weather like this.' He reached into his wallet and pulled out £20. 'Just take this and stay home and dry.'

'I'm not busking,' I said. 'I'm doing a rehearsal with the Royal Opera House Orchestra.' He reddened with embarrassment and we both started to talk at once. Fortunately, the train arrived and we both headed for different doors.

PAVAROTTI IN THE RAIN AND THE SUN

In July1991, I did a concert with the Philharmonic Orchestra – 'Pavarotti in Hyde Park'. He was the soloist and it was attended by an audience which included people who were even more recognisable than he was, among them John Major, the Prime Minister, Prince Charles and Princess Diana, with 125,000 punters watching it in the park on huge screens. It was one of the wettest nights of the summer. A couple of our music critics likened the concert experience to 'Sitting at the bottom of your garden in the pouring rain, watching the concert in your house, through your patio doors on a small television.'

But Pavarotti was on wonderful form and his performance as Des Grieux from *Manon Lescaut* was sublime. Gazing at the Princess and singing Mascagni's words, 'Never was a girl so lovely', was poignant. Diana, drenched to the bone, had never looked lovelier. And Pavarotti had never sounded better.

For a change the orchestra sat under cover, while the VIPs sat in the torrential rain. They weren't allowed to put up their umbrellas as this blocked the view of the people behind them. We had the best seats for once, and an excellent fee.

Sadly, the event ended on a bit of a sour note. Pavarotti had donated his fee to charity, and the tabloids were asking why the orchestra wasn't doing the same, as was often the case with such events. What the press failed to report was that Pavarotti would receive tens of thousands of pounds in royalty payments, which the musicians wouldn't.

We repeated the same concert in Athens at the Herodes Atticus stadium. It was great playing in the open air under a starry sky with no rain. Before the concert a small hut had been erected by the side of the stage as a makeshift dressing room for Pavarotti. He had a lot of trouble managing steps, so couldn't do the long walk on and off the stage between numbers. Having put up the hut, two men then ceremoniously carried the smallest potty you have ever seen into it. The trombone player next to me was shaking with laughter, obviously picturing Pavarotti's huge bottom sitting on a potty made for a very small child.

Just before the concert began, a huge handbag fight started in the audience. Due to administrative miscalculations or possibly ticket touts, many of the best seats had been sold twice. As the audience came into the arena, altercations broke out. There are few things more frightening than determined Greek ladies wielding their handbags with intent. Beware Greeks bearing handbags!

The concert started late.

JESSYE NORMAN IN FRANCE

I had an early start for a two-day trip to France with the Philharmonia Orchestra. I opened the family passport drawer, picked up my wife's passport by mistake, put it back, then grabbed the one that I thought must be mine. I got to the airport at 7.30 a.m., found the orchestra, and joined them in the passport queue. I was engrossed in a conversation with a colleague, when I handed my passport over. As it was handed back, I looked at it and realised that it belonged to my 14-year-old daughter. There were two photographs of her, the first when she was six years old, the second taken when she was aged 14 and had a punk hairdo.

I had two choices: either tell the customs man about my mistake, knowing I might end up missing the day's rehearsal and concert, or pretend I hadn't noticed. Realising that owning up might inconvenience the whole orchestra, I decided to keep quiet. We got to France, I crossed my fingers, and handed my daughter's passport over. It was duly inspected and returned with a French shrug, but without comment. I breathed a sigh of relief. We went to the rehearsal, had a short break, then we played the concert. It turned out to be a hugely memorable night for all the right reasons.

Sir John Pritchard was conducting, and Jessye Norman was singing Strauss's *Four Last Songs*. The magic began with the opening chords and didn't stop. It was if John Pritchard had tied invisible threads from the ends of his fingertips to everyone in the orchestra and somehow combined this with his total empathy with Jessye Norman, who was at her glorious best. The last of the four songs – 'Beim Schlafengehen' ('When falling asleep' – 'is this sleep or death?') faded and there was a palpable silence for a few seconds. Then the audience leapt to its feet. She took ten curtain calls, sailing as a graceful calm presence across the stage. The shouts of 'encore' got progressively louder. Then she stopped and stood as still as a statue. Looking straight into the audience, she gave a radiant smile, shook her head, almost sadly, and slowly left the stage. Her exit remains the most perfect end to a performance I have ever seen.

When we landed in London the next day, there was a delay at customs and to pass the time, the band did a show-and-tell of passport photos. Clearly no one could top mine. Amazed the French had let me in, my fellow musicians pushed me to the front of the queue so they could watch what they fully expected to be an entertaining encounter. I approached a tough-looking customs man. I handed him my daughter's passport with trepidation. He looked at it very carefully then handed it back to me without a word. There was a lot of laughter from the band – I quickly walked away.

CHAPTER 13

TWO TRUMPET TALES

1. MAHLER'S 5TH

The Philharmonia Orchestra were giving a concert at the Royal Festival Hall (RFH), and the second half was Mahler's 5th Symphony. This symphony starts with a trumpet solo and is an extremely tense moment for the player, as even the slightest split or fluffed note will be noticed by everyone in the hall. The 1st trumpet was the orchestra's very fine David Mason, famously known for playing the piccolo B flat trumpet solo on the Beatles' 'Penny Lane'.

For large symphonic or operatic works, the principal trumpet, horn and trombones often have a 'bumper'. This means that the loud 'tutti' (unison passages) can be played by the bumper in order to save the principal player's lips for the solos. David's bumper was Elgar (Gary) Howarth, the principal trumpet of the Royal Philharmonic Orchestra (RPO), who went on to have a very successful career with the Philip Jones Brass Ensemble (PJBE), both as composer and a conductor. Gary was a big man with a good sense of humour and on the whole, he had a calm disposition. However, I had seen him lose his temper once and it had been a frightening sight.

After the interval the orchestra went back on stage. The trumpets were subdued, out of respect for David, knowing that he had an anxious time immediately ahead. The trumpets were seated at the very back of the stage right in front of the choir stalls, which were occupied by the audience.

Just before the leader and the conductor came on stage, a man in the front row of the choir stalls leaned over and tapped David Mason on the shoulder with his rolled-up newspaper and spoke. 'I believe this is a very difficult solo for you, so every time you make a mistake, I will tap you on the head with my newspaper.'

Gary stood up to his full height, looked the man straight in the eye, and said, 'If you move so much as a muscle during any part of this performance, I will not be responsible for my actions.'

The man looked terrified; he had thought he was being a 'character'. At the end of the concert as the applause began, he was nowhere to be seen.

2. SHOSTAKOVICH'S 5TH

I hadn't played Shostakovich's 5th Symphony for many years; not since I had been at college in fact. I was looking forward to it.

The brass feature heavily in many parts of the symphony. We were playing one of these weighty passages in the first movement and the conductor, Gennady Rozhdestvensky, was waving for more sound from the 1st trumpet, who was a good lyrical player but not known for his great fortissimos. Rozhdestvensky stopped and said to the trumpet player, 'I need much more from you.' We started again, and he waved for much more sound from the trumpet, then he stopped again. 'First trumpet, I need you to dominate the whole orchestra. Louder.' The orchestra started the passage again, but with the same result. He stopped again. 'First trumpet, you are supposed to be a Russian tank; you sound like a bicycle.' After this, the player concerned was sometimes referred to as 'the trick cyclist'.

JOHNNY MORRIS

I had been asked to play *Tubby the Tuba* in Belfast with the Ulster Orchestra for a televised Christmas concert. Brydon (Jack) Thomson was conducting and the narrator was Johnny Morris. I had admired Johnny Morris since childhood. He had made lots of great TV programmes for children, including *Animal Magic* – my favourite – and a travel programme for Radio 4 called *Johnny's Jaunts*. He would travel around the world with his imaginary friend Tubby. It was full of wise and witty observations and I was looking forward to meeting him in person.

I had to carry my tuba to Belfast. Security was tight, as it was during the Troubles. At the airport I had to take my tuba out of its case and stand back while security shone a light down the bell and tubing. I was asked to take the instrument to pieces – a time-consuming job I wanted to avoid. Feeling that the easiest way to demonstrate that my tubes weren't blocked – and as it was three days before Christmas – I played them 'Ding Dong Merrily On High', explaining that if anything had been put into the tubing the instrument wouldn't play. At all of the many security checks, they seemed happy about this and it saved me a lot of time and trouble taking my tuba to pieces.

My last security check was at the Belfast International Hotel, where they were especially strict – not surprising as the hotel was apparently the most bombed hotel in the world. We did the rehearsal and had a break before the concert.

Tubby the Tuba was written by George Kleinsinger and Paul Tripp. It was about an orchestra where all the instruments had lovely tunes to play, with the exception of Tubby the Tuba. After the rehearsal, when he gets laughed at by the whole orchestra, Tubby feels rejected and lonely, and goes to sit by the riverside. He is befriended by a bullfrog, who teaches him a tune to sing. In the end he gets to sing the frog's tune and is admired by the orchestra. 'Fine musician that tuba.' It was made famous by Danny Kaye, and became a regular on *Children's Hour*.

Johnny told me later that he had done the narration for the piece on many occasions, and I think to give his life a bit more variety, he had written another piece for orchestra/narrator called *Delilah the Contented Cow*.

Just before the concert Johnny said, with his usual smile, 'Feeling OK, Jim?'

I said I was fine, but a bit nervous.

He took me to one side and produced a big hip flask of Famous Grouse Whisky. 'Here, have a good swig of this.'

I said that much as I would love to, I couldn't really drink before playing. That didn't stop Johnny, who tucked in.

The concert started and seemed to be going well. I was sitting in the front of the orchestra, next to Johnny and the conductor. My word cues were printed on my part just before I had to play, and were given to me by the conductor. I was waiting for my next word cue. As the camera got closer, I heard Jack Thompson say 'shit' under his breath. I began to realise that Johnny had deviated from his narration of *Tubby the Tuba*, into his narration of *Delilah the Contented Cow*. We froze for what seemed an age, then Johnny was suddenly back to Tubby. At the end we took a bow and he signalled to me to follow him into his dressing room. He handed me his hip flask; I took a large swig. He laughed: 'Sorry about that.'

The following day we had to get the first flight back. I had had a late night with some mates and wasn't feeling particularly fresh. Johnny was smiling, and greeting everyone with a cheery 'Good morning', which cheered us all up. I asked him how he did it.

'Well, I poured myself a nightcap before going to bed last night, but I didn't manage to drink it. It was on my dressing table when I woke up this morning, so I thought *Shame to waste it*, so I didn't.'

He was a lovely man, and I wished I had talked to him more. I suppose I felt a bit tongue-tied, in the presence of my boyhood hero. Sadly, I never met him again.

CHAPTER 14

PENULTIMATE

I did a recording of *La Traviata* with Pavarotti and Joan Sutherland. Joannie would sit quietly in her shawl during her bar's rest, doing her knitting and looking like your favourite auntie. Then she would put down her knitting, quietly stand up, and fill every nook and cranny of the huge barnlike Kingsway Methodist Hall with her astonishing voice.

Musicians respond instantly to good playing and singing. I was reminded of a concert I had played in Vienna, with a period orchestra, the Vienna Academy Orchestra.

The concert consisted of short popular pieces (known as lollipops) for the top managers of Shell Oil. It lasted about forty minutes and we played for them just before they ate their meal. There were two arias from Rossini's opera *The Barber of Seville*. The first singer was a perfectly good Austrian baritone who sang 'Largo al factotum' – the barber's song. The orchestra accompanied without much enthusiasm, and there was the usual polite applause.

The next singer was not well known at the time. A pretty young woman came on stage; the orchestra started playing; she smiled and started singing 'Una voce poco fa' (There's a voice that I enshrine). It was wonderful. The strings sat up straight and played with much fuller sounds, and the whole thing took off.

The singer was Cecilia Bartoli.

A great soloist will always lift an orchestra, no matter how tired the musicians are. So understandably I have loved playing my cimbasso in Italian operas with Antonio Pappano. He has a wonderful inner understanding of these works.

SOUNDTRACKS

Musicians' names often appear at the very end of the credits in a film. Everyone has a role to play in making a film, but is the key grip operator or hairdressers' assistant more important than the music score? I am sure that the odd bad hairstyle could be overlooked, but I don't think *Star Wars*, *Lord of the Rings*, the Bond movies or pretty much any film, come to that, could manage without a musical score.

It is reassuring, in this age of advanced technology, that video games are often accompanied by orchestras. Essentially a 19th-century ensemble is being used for 21st-century purposes. The creators – usually teenagers – are often listening in the studio while we play, marvelling at these orchestral sounds that they have never heard before. Long may it continue.

I was travelling to Birmingham early one morning to do some rehearsals and a concert with the City of Birmingham Symphony Orchestra (CBSO). I was in the so-called quiet carriage, which was full of people in suits, working at their laptops, or speaking loudly on their mobiles. A lot of the conversations seemed to be about buying people out, asset-stripping and striking hard bargains.

I was watching the narrowboats going slowly up the Grand Union Canal and slightly envying them, but, I reflected, I was going to join an orchestra to play some lovely music by Elgar as well as I could, with other people who would be doing the same.

Now I know that the world needs fund managers, but I was pleased I wouldn't be spending my day with people who wanted to buy me out, or strip my assets.

THE POWER OF LIVE MUSIC

I met up with the daughter of a colleague, whose father and I had been in the BBC together. She was teaching music to pre-school kids and we had enrolled our son in one of her classes. She asked me if I ever played at the Royal Opera House in Covent Garden. I told her that I worked there regularly. It transpired that she had a passion for ballet, although she hadn't seen any for a long time.

I was about to start playing a run of Prokofiev's ballet *Romeo and Juliet* at the 'Garden', so I offered her a dress rehearsal ticket. We met at the stage door, I gave her a ticket and we arranged to meet after the show.

I came out after the performance to find her, but she wasn't there. I went back into the theatre to look and eventually found her sitting alone in the stalls. As I approached her, I saw she was quietly crying. 'Are you OK?' I asked.

She nodded. 'Sorry I didn't meet you. I had just forgotten how beautiful a live orchestra sounds, playing this sublime music.'

CHAPTER 15

FERMATURE

As a player I have reached the stage of being semi-required. I realise this has to happen. Out with the old, in with the new: the many great younger players who are the future of music. Nonetheless I am finding it hard. Of late, when I have played with good orchestras, I haven't always felt comfortable – I have got out of the habit I suppose.

A famous rugby player who was nearing the end of his career was asked if not being fit enough to play matches troubled him. He said that his fitness was fine, but he felt he was losing his ability to know 'where he was on the pitch without looking'. I feel something similar: I am losing my familiarity with playing in orchestras. People ask 'What did you do for a living?' rather than 'What do you do?' My time as a player is falling into the past, but I remain a musician.

Clive James once wisely said, 'Only a curmudgeon would expect the party to stop when he leaves it.' I have spent many years being a part of wonderful profession, and met many great musicians. It has been a privilege. Musicians come in all types, shapes and sizes, but while we're playing, we function as a unit, all making split-second decisions as one, somehow acting as a collective intelligence. When players have a solo, or a particularly difficult passage, everyone wants it to be good; we have all been there and we know.

The great and good conductors and players make it all worthwhile. Musicians always make the second-rate conductors sound much better than they deserve, while great conductors make the orchestra sound much more than the sum of its parts. That silent, tiny baton controls, unites and enables us to create something magical.

While we are making music, we are the purveyors of truth. Musicians of course aren't any more honest than the rest of the population, but when music is being made, we are all involved in reproducing a work created by a great composer, sometimes even a genius, as perfectly as we can.

As I now have more time, it does leave me free to listen to music; perhaps even to write a book about the music profession...

I have joined a choir; I am enjoying my singing and have started to do some solo recitals. I feel the same as I did at the beginning of my music-making. I have so many things I want to do. I will always be able to recall and replay my best concerts in great detail in my head and I am still loving my journey of discovery. Somehow in these tragic Covid times, music seems even more important.

Here's to music.

A HISTORY OF THE TUBA

The tuba is a large brass instrument of bass pitch. The earlier picture below of me with my tuba was used in the *Oxford Junior Companion to Music in 1973*. All tubas have a conical bore, which makes a rounded sound. Trumpets and trombones have a cylindrical bore, which makes a brighter sound.

To produce a sound on any blowing instrument, one of two things is needed – either a reed to vibrate the air, as with the oboe or clarinet, or a vibration of the lips, as with the French horn, trumpet, trombone and tuba. To change the pitch, you need to tighten and loosen the lips. This gives the player just a few notes on any length of tubing. For the purposes of this chapter, I will talk about brass instruments, but they can be made of wood, large conch shells, horn, metal, or anything that it is hollow.

Large tuba-sized instruments were made by the Romans as long ago as 100 BC. These had been a fixed length of tubing the Tuba Corva, also called the Roman Trumpet). By vibrating their lips, players could only produce a few, but probably mighty, notes to scare their enemies, or for signalling, or even for blowing down the odd wall.

These early blown instruments had a variety of uses. At the synagogue the shofar was traditionally used for various parts of Jewish services. At Rosh Hashanah, the Torah exhorts everyone to 'Wake, you sleepers, from your sleep and you slumberers from your slumber, and atone for your sins.' The shofar is traditionally a ram's horn, but sometimes a kudu or antelope horn is used - a kudu horn shofar).

More enterprising inventors learned that by making holes at strategic places in a piece of tubing, different notes could be played. As the makers acquired more skills, lots of instruments began to be made, either of wood or metal, and often in weird and wonderful shapes. The first of these instruments that could play a variety of notes was the cornett (not to be confused with the brass band cornet). This was a wooden instrument with holes in it. By covering different holes on the instrument, a full two-octave scale could be produced. It was about this time (in the 1400s) that the first evidence of a serpent was found. The serpent was a longer version of a cornett with six holes in it. It was called a serpent because of its snake-like shape. My serpent is a copy of an original English church serpent. These were used in smaller churches to accompany the choir to help them stay in tune. Only the grander churches could afford organs. The later serpents had keys which made the instrument easier to play.

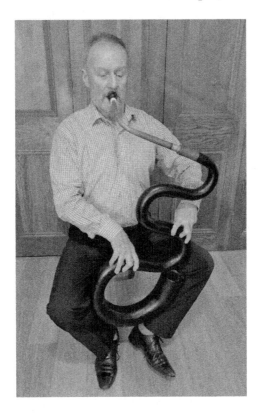

My serpent was made for me by a retired engineer, a wonderfully eccentric man called Christopher Monk. It was made of walnut wood, which was covered in leather. He said he would make it for me provided that I agreed to play it at St John's Smith Square – he was hoping to get the largest serpent gathering ever. He succeeded: 69 serpents and one ophicleide. The programme included the *1812 Overture* and 'Tortoises' from Saint-Saëns's *Carnival of the Animals*. We learned later that he was suffering from cancer and it had been his ambition to get this 'mass serpent gathering' together before he died.

In rehearsal for Mendelssohn's Elijah with the Orchestra of the Age of Enlightenment

Among many notable inventors of wind instruments was Adolf Sax, who made the saxophone. This was a keyed instrument but was blown using a reed. Sax and many more instrument makers had also designed valves for brass instruments. When used they added extra bits of tubing to the original length, so producing lower notes when the valves were pressed. When reliable valves began to be manufactured, trumpets, cornets, horns and tubas began to be made using this new technology.

Different makers produced a whole range of different weird and wonderful instruments: for instance, an ophicleide, which had keys but was blown using the lips. I took part in a performance of Mendelssohn's *Elijah* by the Orchestra of the Age of Enlightenment, in the marvellously refurbished Birmingham Town Hall. I played my ophicleide, but for authenticity a contrabass ophicleide was added.

It is easy to assume that as new instruments were made, they would automatically be used by the players of the day, but players were reluctant to change their instruments and this often led to a strange mixture of different types of instrument being played at the same performances.

This is nicely demonstrated by an article written by George Bernard Shaw. He was the music/opera critic of *The Times* for ten years. He wrote this review, entitled 'Siegfried at Covent Garden', on 15 June 1892 after a visit to the Royal Opera House.

'The darkness was audible as well as visible; for there was no mistaking that cavernous music, with tubas lowing like plutonian bullocks. In that vast mass of brass, it seemed to me that instead of three distinct and finely contrasted families of thoroughbred trombones, horns and tubas, we had a huge tribe of mongrels, differing chiefly in size. I felt that some ancestor of the trombone had been guilty of a mésalliance with a tuba; that each cornet, though itself already a half-bred trumpet, was further disgracing itself by a leaning towards the flugel horn; and that the mother of the horns must have run away with a whole military band.'

Giuseppe Verdi didn't like the tuba being used for bass parts in most of his operas. This is an extract of a letter he sent to his publisher Giulio Ricordi in 1872, just before the performance of *Aida* at La Scala, Milan.

> 'I wish to insist once again on a fourth trombone – that a tuba is just not possible. Talk to Faccio [the conductor]. He should maybe consult with the 1st trombone in order to decide what should be done. I would prefer a trombone basso, which is of the same family as the others; but if this is too difficult to play, then get one of those ordinary ophicleides. In other words, get whatever you like, but not that devilish tuba which will not blend with the others.'

Nowadays nearly all opera companies use a cimbasso for their Verdi, Bellini and Donizetti operas. The cimbasso is essentially a contrabass valve trombone. Its rasping low register has proved very popular with film composers. I played a cimbasso in the first film ever scored for one –*Indochine* (*Indo-China*), starring Catherine Deneuve. Many films have followed, some using up to four cimbassos, plus massed bass trombones and tubas.

I have several tubas; my regular one is an EEb Boosey and Hawkes. As I did quite a lot of testing work for them, I was lucky enough to be able to choose one of their best instruments. I do also have an EEb left-facing bell tuba, which is 101 years old at the time of writing. I also played my sousaphone on the music for a film session of *Anna Karenina*. The sousaphone was invented by John Philip Sousa, the American march king. He thought they would be easier than the tuba to march with if they could be worn. I suspect that he had never tried. They weighed a ton and on the rare occasion that I played one, I felt that I was going to dislocate my left shoulder. The sousaphones played in US college marching bands are mostly made of plastic – much lighter.

I am indebted to Cliff Bevan for a lot of this information. If you would like to find out more about these instruments, Cliff wrote a wonderful, comprehensively researched book called *The Tuba Family*, published by Piccolo Press.

RECORDING ANECDOTES

The English Chamber Orchestra had asked me to join them to record the music for a film called *Chaplin*. The music was written and conducted by John Barry. About 14 minutes after the start of the film, the young Chaplin is doing an audition for Fred Karno, the impresario, played by John Thaw. What could be better to accompany Chaplin's clowning than a tuba solo?

The London Sinfonietta made a recording with Simon Rattle at Abbey Road Studios called *The Jazz Album*. It had a good mix of music, and included a piece called 'San' with a tuba solo *(see Chapter 6)*. I played it again in 1987 at the Proms in the Royal Albert Hall.

I was playing in a small Salvation Army Band for a programme called *Happy Christmas Mr Bean*. We filmed it with Rowan Atkinson in December 1992 and it has been repeated at Christmas many times. *See Chapter 11* for the story of my tuba stunt double.

I was asked to play the sousaphone on a children's TV programme called *Rainbow*. I was to be called 'Mr Oom-pah-pah', and talk to Mr Geoffrey, Bungle and Zippy, then play the shaker while dancing around the kitchen with Rod, Jane, and Freddy *(see Chapter 11)*. If you would like to view me looking fantastically embarrassed, you can see it on *Rainbow Music 1*.

Four of us played in an Italian wedding band in an episode of *Hercule Poirot*. See *Chapter 11* for what the director thought of our looks.

A performance of a ballet I played in at the Royal Opera House, *La Fille Mal Gardée*, was recorded by the BBC for their DVD catalogue: OA0992D. It was conducted by Anthony Twiner and the music is written by Ferdinand Hérold, arranged by Jack Lanchbery. I was playing because the house tuba player was away. There is a tuba solo to accompany the 'village idiot'!

I turned up for a session at Kingsway Methodist Hall, Holborn with the National Philharmonic Orchestra. The conductor was Charles (Chuck) Gerhardt. He had just got onto the rostrum as I was looking at the music and I discovered a tuba solo. Chuck said, 'This looks a bit of a bender for you, would you like to record it now?' I said I would, the light went on and I sight-read the solo. I made one mistake and asked if I could play it again. Chuck said, 'That sounded great, but if you like and we have time we can do it at the end.' We didn't have time; sorry about the mistake.

Classic FM were recording a concert with the Britten Sinfonia, in Canterbury. I was playing the solo part in *Tubby the Tuba*. It went fine and it was going to be broadcast the following week. My wife said she would like to hear it, so we tuned in. At the end of the piece there was an announcement. 'And that was *Tubby the Tuba*, played by the Britten Sinfonia, conducted by Nicholas Cleobury, narrated by Richard Stilgoe.' My wife said, 'They didn't say who the tuba was.' Tongue-in-cheek, I phoned Classic FM. 'I have just heard some really good tuba playing,' I said. 'Could you tell me who it was?' There was a long pause, then the lady answering the phone said, 'I haven't the faintest idea.'

Fame at last!

ACKNOWLEDGMENTS

I should like to say thanks for the patience and encouragement I was given by to Imogen, Magnus, Milo, Dan Jenkins, Catherine Best, Gwyneth H,. Xenia and all of my great colleagues and friends in the world of music. And most importantly my editor and advisor, Andrew Sparke.

Music books also available from APS Books:

ERIC DOUMERC Jamaican Music In England: From the 1960s to the 1990s - A Historical Guide

ERIC DOUMERC The Life and Times of Joseph Hill and Culture

KEITH HORSFALL: Essential Orchestral Works

And in preparation:

ANDREW SPARKE Astor Piazzolla – Maestro Of Nuevo Tango

Printed in Great Britain
by Amazon